COINS OF ANCIENT INDIA

COINS OF ANCIENT INDIA

FROM

THE EARLIEST TIMES

DOWN TO THE

SEVENTH CENTURY A.D.

MAJOR-GENERAL SIR A. CUNNINGHAM

K.C.I.E., C.S.I. R.E.

GYAN

Published by

Gyan Publishing House
5, Ansari Road
Daryaganj, New Delhi-110002
Phone: 011-47034999, 9811692060
E-mail: books@gyanbooks.com

Distribution Network
gyanbooks.com
India, USA, Canada, UK, Australia, France

ISBN : 978-81-212-2546-5 (HB)
First Published, 1891

2nd Impression 2021

Printed at: Gyan Press, Delhi.

Coins of Ancient India
Author: A. Cunningham

COINS

OF

ANCIENT INDIA

FROM

THE EARLIEST TIMES

DOWN TO THE

SEVENTH CENTURY A.D.

BY

MAJOR-GENERAL SIR A. CUNNINGHAM
K.C.I.E., C.S.I., R.E.

LONDON
B. QUARITCH, 15, PICCADILLY.
1891

PREFACE.

THE present work treats of the "Coins of Ancient India" from the earliest times down to the end of the sixth century A.D. The well-known coins of the Satraps of Surâshtra and of the Gupta kings of Magadha are not included, as they have very recently been fully described in the Journal of the Royal Asiatic Society, the former by Pandit Bhagwân Lâl, and the latter by Mr. V. Smith. In a second volume I propose to deal with the "Coins of Mediæval India," from A.D. 600 down to the Muhammadan conquest. This new volume will include (1) the Rajahs of Kashmir; (2) the Shâhis of Gandhâra; (3) the Kulachuris of Chedi; (4) the Chandelas of Mahoba; (5) the Tomaras of Delhi; (6) the Chohâns of Ajmer; with the later coins of (7) the Sisodiyas of Mewâr; and (8) the Pundîrs of Kangra.

Until very lately it was the popular belief that the Indians were ignorant of the art of coinage until the time of Alexander. This popular error I refuted some twenty-five years ago, by quoting the statement of Q. Curtius that Alexander, on his arrival at Taxila, was presented by the Raja with 80 talents of *coined silver* (signati argenti). A similar error is still prevalent regarding Indian sculpture and architecture. Mr. Fergusson was the most strenuous upholder of this view, and his opinion has been very generally accepted. Indeed, the total absence of any examples of either sculpture or architecture which can be assigned with certainty to a date earlier than the time of Asoka, B.C. 350, points undoubtedly to the correctness of Mr. Fergusson's conclusion. But it must be remembered that in those early days, when the country was still covered with forests, nearly all the buildings were made of wood, which was both cheap and easy to work. Even the walls of the royal city of Palibothra were made of wood, as testified by Megasthenes,[1] and also by Euphorion, the librarian of Antiochus III., who describes the *Mauryas* as living in wooden houses:—Μωριεῖς, ἔθνος Ἰνδικὸν, ἐν ξυλίνοις οἰκοῦντες οἴκοις.[2]

Arrian [Indica x.] states that the Indian cities "on the banks of the rivers were built of wood, instead of bricks and mud, to save them from the annual rains and inundations." For the same reason, at the present day, all the towns in lower Burma are built of bamboos and wood, the only brick buildings being the stûpas and temples.

That the Indians were not ignorant of stone masonry is, I think, proved by the name of *Taksha-ṣila-nagara*, or the "cut-stone-city." I am of course aware that other meanings are given to *taksha* by European savants; but that this meaning of "cut" was accepted by the people is shown by the slightly altered form of *Taksha-ṣira* for *Taksha-ṣila*, which gave rise to the Buddhist legend of the "cut-head." This legend is referred to by all the Chinese pilgrims:—by Fa-Hian in A.D. 400, by Sung-yun in A.D. 520, and by Hwen Thsang in A.D. 631. The last

---

[1] Strabo, xv. i., 35, 36.
[2] Steph. Byzant in v. Μωριεῖς.

pilgrim expressly states that "this is the spot where Tathâgata "cut off his head." Fa-Hian also notes that *Chu-cha-shi-lo*, or Takshaṣila, means, in Chinese words, "cut-off-head."

But there is another point which no one has yet noticed, although it has a very important bearing on this architectural question. This point is the simple fact that the Persepolitan style must *certainly* have been previously introduced into India by the Akhæmenian kings of Persia long before the time of Alexander. This point is proved by the prevalence of Persepolitan capitals and bases in every part of the country where remains still exist, from Kâbul eastwards to Bharhut and Buddha Gayâ. As not a single specimen of Greek architecture has yet been found to the east of the Hydaspes, I conclude, with some confidence, that the Persepolitan style must have been introduced during the two centuries of Persian dominion before the time of Alexander.

With regard to the use of sculpture, although no certain examples now remain of an earlier date than the time of Asoka, yet I can point to the statement of Q. Curtius, that an image of Hercules [*Herculis simulacrum*] was carried in front of the army of Porus as he advanced against Alexander.[3] This worship of Hercules is also mentioned by Strabo, on the authority of Megasthenes, as prevailing in the plain country, while the people of the hills worshipped Bacchus.[4] The *Sibæ* are especially noted as worshippers of Hercules, because they wore skins and carried clubs.[5] Judging from their name and dress I conclude that *Ṣiva* was their god. But the identification

---

[3] *Vit. Alex.*, viii. 14, 11. [4] *Geogr.*, xv. 1, 58.
[5] *Geogr.*, xv. 1, 8.

of the other god with Bacchus was certainly due to the mistaken translation of his name by the Greeks. According to Khares of Mytilene, the name of the god was Σοροάδειος, which he translated by οἰνοποίος, or the "wine-maker." But his own spelling of the name shows very clearly that the original was *Sûrya-deva*, the "sun-god," and not *Surâ-deva*, the "wine-god." Philostratus mentions a temple of the sun inside the city of Taxila.[6]

From these examples we see that the Indians already possessed figures of their gods as early as the time of Alexander. It may be argued that these figures were most probably made of wood; and in the case of the *simulacrum* of Hercules that was borne in front of the army of Porus, I should think that it must have been of wood. The custom of carrying images of the gods in procession may have been derived from the Persians, as Strabo relates that on his visit to the joint temple of the Persian deities, Anaïtis, Omanus, and Anadatus, in Cappadocia, he saw a *wooden* statue of Omanus carried in procession.[7]

With reference to the name of *Gandharian Alphabet*, which I have proposed for the native characters found on all the coins of the Greek princes of India, and which I thought might be the *Kharosti* script, which was read from right to left, I have since seen that Dr. G. Bühler has actually made the same identification.[8] He spells the name *Kharoshtri*, a form which seems to offer a strong support to its identification with the name of Zoroaster or *Zarathushtra*, which Burnouf translated as the possessor of "yellow camels." The Chinese translated *Kharosti* by

---

[6] *Athenæus*, i. 48. [7] *Geogr.*, xv. 3, 15.
[8] *Epigraphia Indica*, part vii., p. 384, n. 73.

"ass's lips"; but Dr. Bühler's reading of *ushṭra* seems to point even more closely to the identification with Zoroaster. Both *zarath* and *zar* are connected with the Sanskrit *swarṇa* = "gold." In ancient Persia the Indian *sw* was generally changed to *kh*, as in S. *Saraswati* = Per. *Harakhaiti*, and Greek *Arakhôtos*. *Kharoshṭra* might, therefore, have been a variant form of the name of *Zara-thushtra*. In fact I recognise *khar* in the Greek χρυσός. In the meantime I retain the name of Gandharian as an appropriate and descriptive title for the alphabet which was in common use throughout Gandhâra for about five centuries, from B.C. 250 to A.D. 250. The latest dated inscription which can be read with any certainty is dated in Ṣ. 122 = 200 A.D.[9] Not a single Gandharian letter occurs on the coins of Vâsu-deva or his successors—the only native letters being purely Indian Devanâgari.

---

[9] *Archæological Survey of India*, v., Pl. XVI., fig. 4.

CONTENTS.

			PAGE
Preface.			
Early Names of Coins			1
Connexion of Phœnicia and India			3
Assyria and Babylonia			7
Connexion of India and Persia			12
Persia			13
Assyrian and Babylonian Weights			15
Lydian System			16
Earliest Coinage			19
Talents of the Ancient World			26
The Gandharian Alphabet			31
The Indian Alphabet			38
Coins of Ancient India			42
Punch Coins (*see Frontispiece*, Plate A).	Plate	I.	54
Coins of Taxila	,,	II. and III.	60
Coins of Odumbara	,,	IV.	66
Coins of Kuninda and Kosambri	,,	V.	70
Coins of Yaudheya	,,	VI.	75
Coins of Panchala	,,	VII.	79
Coins of Mathura	,,	VIII.	85
Coins of Ayodhya	,,	IX.	90
Coins of Ujain	,,	X.	94
Coins of Eran, or Erakaina	,,	XI.	99
Coins of the Andhras, S. India	,,	XII.	102
Coins of Nepal	,,	XIII.	112
Map	,,	XIV.	118

COINS OF ANCIENT INDIA.

Early Names of Coins.

In all countries the common measures have been derived from natural objects:

Measures of *length* from fingers, palms, feet, cubits and paces.

Measures of *weight* from seeds and beans, as the *rati* and barley-corn and the *mâsha* and *gerah* beans.

Measures of *capacity* from the handful and double handful, and from the skins of animals[1].

Measures of *time* from the sun and moon.

Coins, of course, deal chiefly with weight, the only exceptions that I am aware of being the Greek δραχμή, which is said to mean a "handful," and to be derived from δράσσομαι, to hold—and the Indian *paṇa*, a "handful" derived from *pâṇi*, the hand. The Greek handful may

[1] The *hide* and the *ox-hide* I may note as measures of land, not according to the old tradition by cutting the hides into strips, but by sewing them up and using them as bags or sacks for holding grain. The piece of land which took a *hide* full of seed would be called a *hide* of land. The *ox-hide* I would suggest as the original form of the present absurd *hogshead*. Both ox-hides and goat-skins are used in India for carrying water. The substitution of *hogs* for *ox* must be a cockney emendation.

have been 48 *chalki*, or copper coins; but the Indian *paṇa* was a handful of cowree shells, usually reckoned as 80. This term *păn* is still used in Bengal, where a *păn* of cowree shells consists of 20 *gaṇdas*, or "20 fours" of cowrees. By repeated trials I have found that 80 cowrees form a very fair average handful. But the *paṇa* was also a copper coin of 80 *rati* seeds in weight (144 grains) and 80 cowrees in value. The Indian reckoning was therefore as follows:—

4 cowrees	= 1 *ganda*, or "four," from *gaṇ*, "to count."	
20 gandas	= 1 *paṇa*	= 144 grs. of copper.
4 paṇas	= 1 *tangka*, or *ana*	= 14 grs. of silver.
4 tangkas	= 1 *kâhan*, or *kârsha*	= 56 grs. of silver.

The weight of the *tangka* is said to have been fixed from the weight of the *mâsha* or "broad bean," which, as I have shown elsewhere, averages 14·6 grains, thus agreeing very closely with the *gerah* of the Hebrews.

The Indian *Kârshâpaṇa* is mentioned by Hesychius under the name of κορσίπιον νόμισμα παρ' 'Αιγυπτίοις, τὸ κερσαῖον λεγόμενον, and in another place he calls the κέρσα 'Ασιανὸν νόμισμα. I have before proposed to alter παρ' 'Αιγυπτίοις to παρὰ Γυπτίοις, thus referring the coins to the time of the Guptas.

Another Indian coin mentioned by a Greek author is the κάλτις of the Periplus. The coin, he says, was of gold νόμισμά τε χρυσοῦ, ὁ λεγόμενος κάλτις, and to this coin he most probably refers, when in another place he says that "gold and silver denarii were exchanged with profit for native money. The *Kaltis* I take to be a gold *hûn* of the weight of a *Kalutti* seed, about 50 grains. It was the native gold currency of the country.

The name of *dramya* or *dramma*, which is found both

in books and in inscriptions, was no doubt derived from the Greeks of the Punjab. It is found in an inscription from Jaunpur of A.D. 1216, as the *shad-vodrikadramya* or the "drachm of six vodris," which certainly refers to the Greek drachm of 6 *oboli*. In another inscription from Besâni of A.D. 1207, I find mention of two sums of 30 *dramas* and 100 *dramas*.

According to Herodotus the earliest stamped money was made by the Lydians. If any earlier coins had existed either in Babylonia or Assyria we should have found some notice of them in the Contract Tablets of Nimrud. But the first mention of purified and stamped pieces is in the reign of Kambyses. The pieces of silver are stated to be "stamped for giving and receiving," that is for currency. They were, undoubtedly, posterior to the Lydian coins, from which they were copied. But all of these early coins of Persia, Lydia, and Greece, were thick, rough, globular pieces of metal. The Corinthians alone made quite flat silver coins, but no reason is assigned for their departure from the common practice of the other peoples. India alone possessed flat pieces of stamped silver of a fixed weight, which in the early Buddhist Sutras were already known by the name of *purâṇa* or "old." The Jâtaka stories certainly speak of these coins as current during the lifetime of Buddha, or from 600 to 543 B.C. The pieces themselves were certainly not copied from any of the other existing coinages.

CONNEXION OF PHŒNICIA AND INDIA.

Owing to their happy position on the narrow neck of land which joins Africa and Asia, the Phœnicians naturally monopolised all the trade of the ancient world between the East and West. Their ships exchanged the silver plates of Tarshish for the gold dust of Ophir, and the merchants of Tyre became princes, and her traffickers the honourable of the earth.[2] From Ophir they brought gold and ivory, apes and peacocks, all productions of India even at the present day. Ophir, or Σωφίρ as in the LXX. version, was almost certainly the country on the lower Indus, called *Sindhu-Sauvîra* by the Indian geographers. It was the Σαβειρία of Ptolemy and *Iberia* of the Periplus. That peacocks were actually carried from India to the west we learn from the *Bâveru-Jâtaka*, translated by Prof. Rhys Davids.[3] *Bâveru* is identified with Babylon, the Bâbirush of the inscriptions of Darius. But the Phœnicians must have traded as far east as Burma and Siam, as the silver unit of traffic in both of those countries, called *tikal*, weighs exactly 224 grains. The name is not a native one, and is said to have been introduced by foreigners. The name alone would be of little interest, but when coupled with the exact weight of the Semitic *shekel*, it seems to me to be a very curious survival.

The Phœnician unit, a small piece of 56 grains, or ¼ Hebrew shekel, may also be connected with the old Indian money unit, the silver *kârsha* of 56 or 57 grains. The silver *kârsha* or *kârshâpaṇa*, was the only coin of the Hindus for many centuries. I venture to call it a coin because every piece that I have seen was certainly stamped, not, it is true, with one large die, but with several small punches. Some pieces have only a few marks, while many

---

[2] Isaiah xxiii. 8.

[3] *Babylonian and Oriental Record*, iii. 7.

have only one mark on the reverse. Their exact agreement in weight can scarcely be accidental, and as India produces very little silver, I presume that the Phœnicians brought the silver plates of Tarshish to exchange for the gold dust of India. The gold of Ophir is described by Job[4] as "dust of gold" or "particles of gold," which is the very form in which it was obtained by Darius, and in which I have myself obtained it from the washings of the Indus. It is, besides, specially worthy of notice that throughout the vast extent of the Persian empire, India was the only satrapy that paid its tribute in gold. All the other nineteen satrapies, from the shores of the Aegean Sea to the banks of the Indus, paid their tributes in silver. India, in fact, produced little or no silver, while gold was abundant. Herodotus describes the Indian gold as gathered from the sands of Paktuike.[5] Hence amongst the Afghans, or people of Paktuike, silver was only known as "spin-zar," or white gold. The gold dust of India is also noted by Megasthenes as being sold to the merchants in its natural state, because it did not require to be purified.[6] It is also mentioned that the merchants made a profit by exchanging their own money for Indian gold.[7] Gold was cheap in India, being as 1 to 8 rates of silver, whereas in Persia the rate was 13 of silver. I infer that the Indian gold dust was usually kept in its natural state, in small packets of fixed weight. It is, perhaps, to this practice that Isaiah refers when he says "they lavish gold *out of the bag*, and *weigh* silver with the balances."[8] Jeremiah also points to the East as the source of gold, and to the West as that of silver, when he

[4] Job xxviii. 6—16.

[5] III. 102.

[6] *Strabo*, XV. i. 44.

[7] Periplus, pp. 123—127.

[8] Ch. xlvi. 6.

speaks of "silver *beaten into plates* brought from Tarshish, and gold from Uphaz (or Ophir).[9]

From all these facts I feel convinced that the gold of Ophir, which was known to Job as dust, and which was brought by Phœnician ships to David and Solomon, must have been obtained in India. The annual tribute of India to Persia was certainly paid in gold dust, and I think it is only natural to infer that this was a simple continuance of the old flow of Indian gold from east to west.

If the *kârsha* is the representative of the Phœnician small *shekel* of 56 to 57·5 grains, and the *tikal* of Burma and Siam is the representative of the large *shekel* of 224 to 230 grains, it follows that the *vis* of 100 *tikals,* which is used in several places on the east coast of India, as well as in Burma, must also be of Phœnician origin—as implied by the round number of 100. The name is neither Indian nor Burmese. The number of 100 tikals recalls the Hebrew *Manah* which contained 50 shekels. The Burmese have slightly altered the name to *pikthay,* in which the soft *th* represents the *s* of *vis.* The Tâmil people call it *visai.*

The name of *kârsha* is probably indigenous, as it is derived from *krish,* to mark or furrow; and all the silver pieces that were current under this name are certainly marked with one or more punch-stamps. But the fabric of these *kârshas,* or *purâṇas* (old) as they were also called, is quite different from the money of any other people. All the most ancient coins that I have seen, with the single exception of Corinth, such as the Crœsics of Lydia, the Darics of Persia, the Electrum Staters and Hektæ of Asia Minor, the Owls of Athens, and the Tortoises of Aegina, are thick round knobs or buttons of metal, which

---

[9] Ch. x. 9.

must have been cast for the particular purpose. The old Indian silver *purâṇas* on the contrary are all flat thin pieces, which have been cut from beaten plates.[10] The two modes of fabrication are so utterly different that it is quite impossible to conceive that one could have been the model for the other. The earliest pieces would have been simple blanks of a fixed weight. I conclude that they were kept in small bags of 25, or 100, or even 1000 pieces. The smaller one of 25 kârshas would have been the equivalent of the gold *suvarṇa* of 140 grains. The suvarṇa also was a simple bag of gold dust, such as is still current in Kumaon of the value of 8 rupees. Each of these gold dust bags is now called *phetâng*, which I take to be a survival of the Rig Veda name of *piṇḍân*, or collected quantities of gold dust.

Assyria and Babylonia.

The Contract Tablets from Kuyunjik and Nimrud, now in the British Museum, are among the most ancient remains of the East that have lately been deciphered. In them we find the record of sales of lands, houses, and slaves, and of loans of money with the interest per month, all detailed in the ancient currency of *manas* and *shekels* of silver. In a few cases the "*mana* of Karkemish" is specially mentioned as if it was a different species from the others. On No. 13 of the Kuyunjik tablets mention is made of intercourse with "Gugu, king of Luddi, or Gyges of Lydia, during the reign of Assurbanipal of

[10] These flat, thin pieces were, perhaps, suggested by the flat plates of silver which were brought from Tarshish, as India possessed no silver of its own. Jeremiah x. 9 describes the silver from Tarshish as beaten (or spread) into plates.

Assyria. Altogether of these Assyrian money tablets there are about 30, ranging in date from B.C. 709 down to 620. Of course there are many other tablets of much older date beginning with Tiglath-Pileser I., B.C. 1120-1100.

The Nimrud Tablets of Babylonia are much more numerous, and cover a much longer period of time. The earliest date from the time of King Risn-sin about B.C. 2130, of King Hamurabi, about B.C. 2120, and of Samsu-iluna, B.C. 2075. A long interval then follows without money records until the time of Esarhaddon in B.C. 677, who held both Assyria and Babylonia. From his reign there is a very interesting series, with the well-known names of Nebuchadnezzar, Cyrus, Kambyses, Darius, Xerxes, several of the Macedonian kings of Syria, ending with the Parthian king, Arsaka, in B.C. 94 and 93. The sums mentioned in these Babylonian tablets are still named *manas* and *shekels*, but there is nothing to show whether they differed from those of Assyria. The first notice of stamped money (real coinage) is found during the reign of Kambyses and Darius I. Apparently three different kinds of money were then in use, (1), common silver pieces without mark; (2), pure or refined silver; and (3), stamped silver. The last coins are specially described as intended for giving and receiving (or buying and selling). (See Tablet No. 97 Nimrud—*B. M. Cat.*)

The ancient weights of Assyria and Babylonia which were found by Layard in the ruins of Nineveh are of two kinds, bronze lions and stone ducks. The former are just double the weight of the latter. The heavier *mina* ranges from a maximum of 16,068 grains down to 14,832, and the lighter mina from 8,034 grains down to 7,107 grains.[11] Dr. Brandis, who is here followed by Mr. Head, assumes the *mean* values of 15,600 and 7,800 grains for these two minæ. But as this low valuation would appear to have been assumed so as to agree with the low weight of 130 grains hypothetically assigned to the Daric, I unhesitatingly reject it. The true original weight of the Daric can be derived from the existing Persian sigli, for which Mr. Head allows a value of 86·45 or 86·5 grains. He quotes Xenophon's value of the siglos as 7½ Attic obols, or 84 grains, but he omits the higher estimate of Hesychius of 8 Attic obols. Taking the Attic obolus at 11·2 grains, these two estimates would be respectively 84 and 89·6 grains, giving an average of 86·8 grains. I am willing, however, to accept Mr. Head's estimate of 86·45 grains. Now we know from Xenophon that the Persian talent contained 300 Darics, and as each Daric contained 20 sigli, the talent was equal to 300 × 20, or 6,000 silver sigli. Multiplying this number of 6,000 by 86·45 we obtain 518,700 grains as the full weight of the Persian talent. Dividing this number by 13, the rate of gold to silver, as given by Herodotus, we get 39,900 grains as the equivalent weight in gold of a talent of silver, and dividing this again by 300 we get 133 grains as the weight of the gold Daric. But to keep down this value to 130 grains it is necessary to alter the text of Herodotus from 13 rates to 13·3. Dr. Brandis and his copyists thus obtain 39,000 grains as the gold equivalent of the talent, which divided by 300 gives 130 grains exactly as the empirical weight of the Daric.

But just as one false step often leads to the necessity of taking a second, so this erroneous assumption of the

---

[11] B. V. Head, *Lydia*, 2.

weight of the Daric leads to the depreciation of the weight of the Corinthian stater down to 130 grains. Now as it is admitted that the Corinthian system was derived from the Babylonians, the adoption of the low weight of 130 grains for the Daric has necessitated the adoption of the same weight of 130 grains for the Corinthian stater, in spite of the well-known fact that the Corinthian coinage maintained the same high standard both in purity and weight as the boasted Athenian coinage. Mr. Head in his later catalogue of the coins of Corinth has now adopted 135 grains as the normal weight of the Corinthian stater.

I have no objection to the *normal* weight of 135 grains for the staters of Athens and Corinth; but I much prefer the slightly lighter weight of 134·4 grains on account of its great convenience. As I have already pointed out in another place,[12] 134·4 is not only a finite number itself, but it is continually divisible by 2 down to 0·7 grains, or the sixteenth part of an obolus. It gives a drachm of 67·2 grains, and an obolus of 11·2 grains. It also gives the whole number of 112 grains for 10 oboli, the stater of Macedon, 56 grains for the drachm of Phœnicia, and 224 grains for the Hebrew shekel, all in whole numbers. It makes the Attic talent equal to 57·6 English pounds, with a finite fraction. At the same time it makes other talents equally compact, and therefore readily convertible into English money.

The heaviest of the bronze *Lions* found at Nineveh has 15 marks on its side, to show that it was 15 *mânas*, or one quarter talent in weight. It weighs only 32·045 lbs. avoirdupois, while the heaviest of the stone *Ducks* is

[12] *Num. Chron.*, 1873, p. 6.

32·77 lbs. The former would give a talent of 128·18 lbs., while the latter would give 135·08 lbs. As this heavier weight agrees very nearly with that of 133·77 lbs. as derived from the ingots of Crœsus, we learn that the Lydians had adopted the Assyrian talent. But it was the weights only which the Lydians borrowed, and in return they gave to the ancient world the invention of stamped coins, which declared the value without the trouble and delay of weighment.

With the Assyrian talent the Lydians would seem also to have accepted its division into sixths, as I find the series of 168, 56, 28, and 14 grains both in gold and in silver. The silver alone has a half coin of 84 grains, which agrees with the Persian siglos both in weight and in fabric. Accepting an approximate weight of 136 lbs. for the heavy Assyrian talent, and one half, or 68 lbs., for that of the Babylonian talent, the following will be the different weights of the two systems:—

	ASSYRIAN.		BABYLONIAN.	
1 talent	136 lbs.	952,000 grs.	68 lbs.	476,000 grs.
1 mâna	2·266 lbs.	15,866 grs.	1·133 lbs.	7,966 grs.
1 siglos	$\frac{1}{60}$	264·4	siglos	132·76 grs.

We have thus obtained the approximate values of the *mâna* and shekel, which are so often mentioned in the Contract Tablets of the Assyrians and Babylonians.

The Eastern origin of the Euboïc and Corinthian systems becomes at once apparent on a comparison of the weights of their coins with those of Lydia and Persia, including the Persian satrapies of Asia Minor. The satrap coins are all double sigli, while the Arabic silver coins of Persia are single sigli. I possess a silver piece of 4 *danakes*, weighing 55·5 grains, or two-thirds of the siglos. The heavy silver pieces ranging up to 433·5 grains I take to be pentasigla, or 5 sigli Persian coins, but I am aware that they have been otherwise described as octadrachms, of 8 Phœnician drachms.

Connexion of India and Persia.

A connexion between Persia and India was established by Darius by his conquest of the Punjab, or districts on both banks of the Indus, from which he drew an annual tribute of "360 talents of gold dust."[13] The historian specially notes that the other 19 satrapies paid their tribute in silver according to the Babylonian talent, while the gold was reckoned according to the Euboïc talent. The Babylonian talent, he adds, contained 70 Euboïc minæ, and he gives the total of the Babylonian money, when reduced to the Euboïc scale, as 9,540 Euboïc talents. The gold dust reckoned at 13 times the value of silver he makes 4,680 talents, and the whole revenue 14,560 Euboïc talents.

There are discrepancies in the numbers of the historian's text, which have puzzled most commentators. His two totals of gold and silver, when added together, do not make his sum total. I solved this difficulty more than thirty years ago (1858). The chief error lies in the valuation of the Babylonian talent at 70 Euboïc minæ. The true value should be 78, as the gold is said to be 13 times the value of silver; that is, as the rate of 10 : 13 :: 60 : 78. The next error is in the valuation of the silver. Deducting 140 talents from the 500 of the fourth satrapy, because that sum was kept for the cavalry

---

[13] *Herodotus*, iii. 94.

and not paid into the treasury, the actual total of the 19 silver paying satrapies was—

7,600 Babylonian talents of 78 Euboïc minæ.
equal to 9,880 Euboïc talents of 60 minæ (not 9,540, [as in text).
add gold 360 × 13 = 4,680 silver.
Total . 14,560 Euboïc talents as given in the text.

We thus see that the total amount agrees exactly with the proportion of 13 silver to 1 gold. I notice this point the more particularly as I see that Mr. Head has adopted the assumed value of 13·3 to 1 as proposed by Mommsen and Brandis.

PERSIA.

As the Persian empire was the successor of the Assyrian and Babylonian monarchies, it naturally inherited and adopted their systems of weights and measures. But as neither of the older kingdoms has left any coins, we can only refer to their heavier weights in the shape of bronze *lions* and stone *ducks,* of which many examples have been found by Layard and others. From these weights it has been discovered that there were two distinct systems in use, of which one was exactly double the other. Many of the weights are inscribed with their values both in cuneiform and in Phœnician characters. The older weights show a heavy *mina* of 16,068 grains, and a light *mina* of 8,034 grains. Dividing both by 60, the unit of the former would be 268 grains, and of the latter 134 grains. But taking the average weights of the *much worn coins,* Dr. Brandis fixed the different *mina* weights at the lower values of 15,600 and 7,800 English grains. These values would give talents of 936,000 and 468,000 grains, or 133·714 and 66·857 lbs. avoirdupois, and units of 260 and

130 grains. Now I am under the impression that these lower values were adopted for the express purpose of bringing the unit of the lighter weight, 130 grains, to accord exactly with the weight of the Daric, as assumed from the much-worn coins.

But I must strongly demur to this low appreciation of the Daric, as it necessitates an arbitrary change in the text of Herodotus, by raising his 13 rates to 13·3 rates of silver to 1 of gold, so as to bring the value of the Daric to agree with 20 silver sigli. Mr. Head makes the weight of the silver siglos 86·45 grains, which, multiplied by 20, gives 1,729 grains of silver as the equivalent of the gold Daric. This amount, divided by the 13 rates of Herodotus, would make the Daric exactly 133 grains in weight. Xenophon makes the value of the Persian siglos only 7½ Attic oboli, or 11·2 grains × 7·5 = 84 grains; but as the greater value of 8 oboli, or 11·2 grains × 8 = 89·6 grains, is given by Hesychius, I am willing to accept Mr. Head's estimate of 86·45 grains as a very fair mean of the two values. I have found 10 good coins give an average of 85·19 grains, the heaviest being 87·90.

It is my belief that the Daric of Persia was the original gold stater from which the Euboïc, afterwards called the Attic, system, was derived. In comparing the weight of the Darics with the staters of Athens and Corinth, we must compare the actual weights of the existing coins of each class, and not take the full normal weights of the Greek coins and the lighter weight of the much-worn Darics, which had been in circulation for centuries. I have examined the catalogues of Hunter and Leake, and, after excluding all coins under 132 grains in weight, I find that 46 staters of Corinth and its colonies give an average of just over 133 grains, while the coins of Athens yield a mean stater of somewhat under 133 grains. As the normal weight of the staters of both Athens and Corinth is usually accepted as 135 grains, the existing specimens show a loss of 2 grains.

The gold coins show even a greater loss of weight. I have taken the weights of 120 gold staters, all over 130 grains, of Philip II., Alexander III., Alexander Aegus, Lysimachus, Seleukus I., and Antiochus I., which give an average of only 131·2 grains. A former weighment of 78 staters of the same princes gave only 132·11 grains; and Hussey, p. 16, records that 71 staters of the same kings gave only a small fraction over 132 grains. It is true that the existing Darics do not reach this average. H. P. Borrell records that he found the average of 125 Darics, which he weighed himself, to be only 129·4 grains.[14] But I possess one of 132·5 grains, and the Duc de Luynes had one of 132 grains. I fully believe, therefore, that the Persian Daric was originally of the same weight as the Euboïc stater. The 4 known Attic staters give a mean of only 131·14 grains, while the 5 heaviest Darics, of which I have a record, give a mean of 131·34 grains.

Assyria and Babylonia.

This brings me to the consideration of the Assyrian and Babylonian weights. Accepting the original weight of the Daric at 133 grains, and that of the silver siglos at 86·45 grains, Mr. Head's own valuation, then the light talent would be 86·5 × 6000 = 518,700 grains, or exactly 74·1 lbs. avoirdupois, and the heavy talent would be just double, or 1,037,400 grains, or 148·2 lbs. Now it is a

---

[14] H. P. Borrell, *Num. Chron.*, vi. 153.

singular fact that in the territories of modern Persia there still exist two systems of weights of which the average of one set is just double that of the other. The following are examples of the two systems :—

Man.		Batman.	
Shâhi Man, Gambrun	13·8 lbs.	Batman, of Tauris	6·34 lbs.
Man, of Bagdad	16·5 ,,	Others . . .	6·75 ,,
Batman, of Cherray	12·6 ,,		7·75 ,,
Shiraz and Bagdad	14·0 ,,		7·73 ,,
		Tabriz and Bushir	6·98 ,,
	56·6 ,,		35·55 ,,
	4		5
Heavy mean	14·14 lbs.	Light mean	7·08 lbs.

The Lydian money is similar to that of Persia, consisting of double and single staters in gold, and double and single sigli in silver. The weights of the coins show that the system must have been received either from Assyria or from Babylonia. Professor Sayce suggests that it was brought by the Hittites of Karkhemish through Phrygia to Lydia. But as we know that Gyges had intercourse with Assyria, Mr. Head very pertinently asks, "Why the lighter weight was used in Lydia?" He quotes Norris's opinion that the lighter weights belonged to Babylonia, and the heavier to Assyria, but thinks that "this cannot be proved." Now the ingots of Crœsus prove incontestably that the Lydian system was the heavy one of Assyria, as suggested by the Lydian intercourse with Assyria.

Lydian System.

The proof that the Lydians adopted their system from Assyria I derive from the weights of the ingots of gold and electrum which were presented by Crœsus to Delphi.[15]

[15] *Herodotus*, i. 50.

According to Herodotus he gave 4 ingots of pure gold and 117 of electrum. Each slab was 6 palms long, 3 palms broad, and 1 palm thick. The gold slabs weighed $2\frac{1}{2}$ talents each, the electrum slabs only two talents. Taking the Greek palm at 3·03375 inches, each slab or ingot contained 502·898 cubic inches, which, allowing ·665 lbs. to each cubic inch of gold, gives 133·771 lbs. as the weight of one talent. Continuing the calculation, it will be found that the electrum talents consisted of 179·99157 lbs. of gold and 87·55448 lbs. of silver, or rather more than two-thirds of gold and rather less than one-third of silver. Now a talent of 133·771 lbs. approaches so closely to the weight of the Assyrian talent, as fixed by Brandis at 133·71 lbs., that I have no hesitation in deriving the Lydian system from that of Assyria. Mr. Norris was therefore right in his opinion.

But the Lydian coins, both gold and silver, seem to me to declare the same origin, as there are double as well as single staters of gold, and double as well as single sigli of silver. I do not, however, accept the weight of the Lydian talent thus derived as being more than a tolerably near approximation, as it appears to me quite incredible that the size of the ingots could have been in exact *whole* numbers of Attic palms as described by Herodotus. A talent of 133·771 lbs. would have given a *silver* double siglos of 156 grains, whereas the few existing coins show that the weights were not less than 164 and 82 grains, which must have been derived from a talent of over 140 lbs. As this agrees very closely with the mean weight of the *dah-man*, or 10 mans which is still in use in Gambrun, Bagdad, and Shiraz, I think that it may be accepted as the Lydian equivalent of the Assyrian weight.

As my numbers differ from those published by Mr. Head in *Num. Chron.*, 3rd Series, VII., 302, I will here give my calculation in detail. He notes that the electrum talents of Crœsus must have contained about 73 per cent. of gold and 27 of silver, whereas my calculation gives 67·3 per cent. of gold and 32·7 of silver. The data given by Herodotus are as follows :—

A—each ingot measured 6 palms by 3 palms by 1 palm.
B—the gold ingot weighed $2\frac{1}{2}$ talents.
C—the electrum ingot weighed 2 talents.

Taking the Attic palm at 3·03375 inches, each ingot contained 502·898 inches. Taking gold at ·665 lbs. per cubic inch, the gold ingot of $2\frac{1}{2}$ talents must have weighed 334·427 lbs., and therefore 1 talent weighed 133·771 lbs. Taking the weight of silver at ·377 lbs. per cubic inch,

$$\left.\begin{aligned}\text{Let } x &= \text{No. of cubic inches of gold}\\ y &= \text{No. of cubic inches of silver}\end{aligned}\right\}\text{ in electrum ingot.}$$

$$\begin{aligned}\text{then 1, } x + y &= 502{\cdot}898 \text{ cubic inches of ingot,}\\ \text{and 2, } {\cdot}655x + {\cdot}377y &= \text{weight of electrum ingot}\\ &= 2 \text{ talents,}\\ &= 2 \times 133{\cdot}771 \text{ lbs.}\\ &= 267{\cdot}542 \text{ lbs.}\end{aligned}$$

$$\begin{aligned}\text{Multiplying 1 by } {\cdot}665\text{, we get } {\cdot}665x + {\cdot}665y &= 334{\cdot}427 \text{ lbs.}\\ \text{and 2} \quad {\cdot}665x + {\cdot}377y &= 267{\cdot}542 \text{ lbs.}\\ \hline {\cdot}288y &= 66{\cdot}885 \text{ lbs.}\end{aligned}$$

$$\therefore y = \frac{66{\cdot}885}{{\cdot}288} = 232{\cdot}240 \text{ cubic inches of silver,}$$

$$\text{and } x = \quad 270{\cdot}658 \text{ cubic inches of gold}$$

$$\text{Total} \quad . \quad 502{\cdot}898 \text{ cubic inches of ingot.}$$

$$\begin{aligned}\text{Then } 232{\cdot}240 \text{ cub. in. silver} \times {\cdot}377 &= 87{\cdot}5545 \text{ lbs. silver,}\\ \text{and } 270{\cdot}658 \text{ cub. in. gold} \times {\cdot}665 &= 179{\cdot}9985 \text{ lbs. gold.}\\ &\quad 267{\cdot}5530 \text{ lbs.} = 2 \text{ talents}\\ 2 &\overline{\quad 133{\cdot}7765 \text{ lbs.} = 1 \text{ talent.}}\end{aligned}$$

$$\left.\begin{aligned}\text{Gold} &= 67{\cdot}3 \text{ per cent.}\\ \text{Silver} &= 32{\cdot}7 \text{ per cent.}\end{aligned}\right\}\text{ electrum.}$$

I find it difficult to believe, if the weights of the Lydian ingots were exactly 2½ talents and 2 talents, as noted by Herodotus, that all their three dimensions of 6 palms, 3 palms, and 1 palm, could by any possibility have been exact whole numbers of the Attic palm. The length of the palm which I have used above is that which has been derived from the platform of the Parthenon at Athens, commonly known as the *Hekatompedon*, of 100 feet front. Stuart's measurements make the Attic foot equal 12·137 English inches and the palm equal 3·033 inches or 3·0345. But if the Attic measure did not quite agree, and was only a very close approximation, a very minute addition of about ·015, or fifteen-thousandths of an inch, to each palm, making 3·050 inches, would increase the weight of the Lydian talent to 135·8 lbs. avoirdupois. Dividing this amount by 3,600, we obtain the full weight of the Assyrian shekel of 264·1 grains, and of 132 grains for the gold coins.

Earliest Coinage.

The earliest coinage of the ancient world would appear to have been chiefly of silver and electrum; the latter metal being confined to Asia Minor, and the former to Greece and India. Some of the Lydian staters of pale gold or electrum may certainly be as old as Gyges, while the rude silver pieces of Argos and Aegina cannot be placed later than the time of Pheidon. By the silver coinage of India I refer to the thousands of square silver pieces which are found all over the country from the Himâlaya Mountains to Cape Comorin, and from Sistân to the mouths of the Ganges. As all these pieces are stamped with several dies or punches, on one or both faces, they have received the descriptive name of punch-marked coins. In the Hindu books they are called *purâṇa,* or "old," a title which vouches for their antiquity. They are mentioned by Manu and Pânini, both anterior to Alexander, and also in the Buddhist Sutras, which are of about the same age. The original name of the coin was *kârshâpaṇa,* from *kârsha,* "a weight," and *âpaṇâ,* "custom or use," meaning that they were pieces of one *kârsha* weight as established by use or custom. In the same way the Greek *νόμισμα* was derived from *νομίζω.* According to Buddhist tradition the *kârshâpaṇa,* or *kâhâpaṇa,* was called *purâṇa* at least as early as the time of Buddha himself. This is shown by the curious story, extracted by Burnouf from the Sutras, of the courtesan Vâsavadattâ, who demanded 500 *purâṇas* as the price of her favours. These Indian ladies must have been as difficult of access as the Greek Hetairæ of Corinth, whose exactions gave rise to the proverbial saying,

Non cuivis homini contingit adire Corinthum.

As Buddha's death is placed in the middle of the sixth century B.C., the silver *purâṇas* of India may be quite as old as any of the coinages of Geeece or Asia Minor. In the frontispiece, Plate A, I have given two pictorial representations of a well-known Buddhist legend regarding the purchase money of the Jetavana garden at Srâvasti. As the story is related at length in my description of the Bharhut Stûpa, p. 84, it will be sufficient to note here that the owner of the garden, Prince Jeta, stipulated that he would only part with it on the condition that the purchaser should cover the whole surface with coins touching each other. Both scenes represent the coins being laid out "edge to edge." It will be seen that the pieces are all square. The older sculpture dates from 250 B.C.

The earliest-known *gold* coins are the Lydian *staters* of Crœsus and the Persian Darics of Darius. The former are very rare, and I have no doubt that they were made by refining the *electrum*, as described by Herodotus. The Persian Darics must have been made from the annual tribute of Indian gold dust which Darius received from the Punjab. Herodotus specially notes that the tribute was paid in "gold-dust."[16] By this I understand that in the end of the sixth century B.C. the Indians had no gold coinage. But they certainly had measures or fixed weights of gold in bags, which passed current amongst the people. The issue of Darics amounted to several millions, as we learn from the story of the Lydian Pythius, who possessed a sum of no less than 4,000,000 of Daric staters, less 7,000. The amount seems almost incredible, especially for a private person. Alexander is said to have found 9,000 talents of Daric staters at Susa, besides fabulous amounts of uncoined gold at Susa, Persepolis, and Pasargada. The Persians, we know, succeeded to the hoarded treasures of the Assyrians and Babylonians. According to Khares of Mitylene, one of the companions of Alexander, a treasure of 5,000 talents of coined gold was kept in the bedchamber of the Persian king.[17] As to the hoarding of treasure, we have proof in the account of the gold and silver vessels carried away from Jerusalem by Nebuchadnezzar, which were still preserved in the treasury at Babylon in the time of Cyrus.

The question naturally arises, "From whence came these large amounts of gold?" I believe that the greater quantity came from India. From the time of David and

---

[16] *Herodotus*, iii. 94 and 96.
[17] *Athenæus*, xii. 514.

Solomon down to Darius, the Phœnicians had been bringing gold from Ophir. In one year they brought 450 talents to Solomon. They traded also for gold with the island of Thasos in the Aegean, and thus for some five centuries gold continued to flow, both from the East and from the West, into the countries on the Euphrates and the Tigris. After the conquest of the Punjab by Darius the Indian gold came for two centuries as an annual tribute into the Persian treasury.

The gold of India has always been noted for its deep yellow hue, from which it has received its common name of *suvarṇa*, that is, *su+varṇa*, or "beautiful colour." For this reason Sophocles, in B.C. 440, in his *Antigone*, contrasts the "gold of India with the electrum of Sardis." *Suvarṇa* at last became the name of a piece of gold, equal in value to 25 silver *kârshas*. At this rate the ratio of gold to silver was 10 to 1, if the *kârsha* be taken at its full weight of 56 to 57·6 grains, or only 8 to 2 if taken at its weight in pure silver of 44·8 grains. As the rate in Persia was 13 to 1, a very fair profit might have been made by exchange—the Persian by getting gold, the Indian by receiving silver. This intercourse might have led to the adoption of some at least of each other's weight names. But this does not appear to have been the case, as the only term common to both peoples is the 14 grain *danake* of Persia, or one-sixth of the siglos, and the 14 grain *tangka* of India, or one-fourth of the *kârsha*. I am inclined to think that the *danake* or *danik* was actually an adopted name, as I find a coin named *ropaka*, which is said to have been one-seventieth of a *suvarṇa*, or 2 grains of gold or the equivalent in silver. I may note, however, that the double silver shekel of Persia and the satrapies, or 86·5 × 2 = 173 grains, agrees exactly with the Indian weight of 100 ratis of 1·75 grains each.

The ancient Persian siglos was divided into 6 *danakes*, just as the modern *mishkâl* is now divided into 6 *dâniks* or *dângs*. The Δανάκη is mentioned by three different authors, Pollux, Hesychius, and Suidas. Pollux writes the name *Danikè*, *Danakè* and *Danikion*, and says that it was a Persian coin. Hesychius calls it *Danaë*, and says that it was worth more than an obolus. But *Danaë* is certainly a mistake for *Danakè*, as he names the half-coin *Hemi-Danakion*. Suidås also writes the name *Danakè*, and repeats what is also said by Hesychius, that it was placed in the mouths of the dead. According to Xenophon the siglos was equal to 7½ oboli; but Hesychius values it at 8 Attic oboli. Taking the Attic obolus at 11·2 grains, the mean of these two values will be 86·8 grains, which agrees so nearly with Mr. Head's 86·45 grains, that I am perfectly willing to accept his value. The danike of one-sixth would therefore be 14·41 grains, which is exactly the weight of the Indian *tangka*. But as the word *tangka* is derived from the *tang* or *twank* sound of metal when struck by a chisel, the name would seem to belong specially to any *stamped* coin. The name therefore meant simply any *stamped* coin; and was applied to several different pieces quite irrespective of their value. At first it was perhaps a simple weight; and after a stamp was added it became the name of a coin. But it was applied to the silver *kârsha*, and also to the copper *pana*, which was also known as a "copper tangka." It soon became a general term for money, and it is so used in the Râja Tarangini as *tangkaka*. It appears on some rare dirhems of Mahmud of Ghazni, with a Sanskrit inscription, the coin being described as *ayam tankam*, or "this tanka." It was in common use during the whole period of Muhammedan rule. In A.D. 1412 the Chinese envoys, who visited Bengal, describe the *silver* coin of the king Ayas-i-ting, or Ghias-ud-din Azem, as a *thang-kia*, weighing 2 thsiam, each $\frac{2}{10}$ of a Chinese ounce, plus *sen* or $\frac{8}{100}$.[18] In the time of Sher-Shah his large copper coins of 124 grains were called *tankah*, and the same name was used by Akbar for his double copper coins of 648 grains. The word has descended down to our own time under the form of *takkâ*, and is frequently used for money in general. Ibn Batuta, A.D. 1340, calls the gold *dinars* of Muhammad Tughlak *tanka*. Silver *tankas* are also noted, and in the time of Bahlol Lodi "black tankas" of copper are mentioned, of which 20 went to the silver *tanka*. But these Bahloli copper coins contained as much as 7 or 8 grains of silver; a score of them was just equal to one white or silver *tanka*.

The same word is also in common use for a four anna piece, or quarter rupee, the silver *Kârsha;* and under the form of "*tanner*," I believe that it has been introduced into England by the gypsies, as a slang name for sixpence.

Considering the continuous use of the name in India, and the simple Indian derivation of the word, I believe that the name is certainly of Indian origin, and that it was perhaps first employed shortly after the old blank silver Kârsha weights were marked with punches, and thus acquired the designation of *tangka*, or "stamped" pieces.

With reference to the square form of the greater number of these old silver coins, I notice that the small *square* piece, which a fruit-seller of the present day cuts out of a melon to show its quality, is called a *tângki*.

---

[18] Pauthier, p. 88.

In the Raja Tarangini this coin is called *Tâka,* where the Queen of Ananta in want of money sells a jewelled lingam for "7 lakhs of Tâkas." Troyer gives the translation correctly (Raja Tar. vii. 415), but the last native translator Bâbu Jogesh Chunder Dutt (kings of Kashmir, p. 198), makes the Queen sell it for "70 lakhs *to* the Tâkâs." The coins were, no doubt, the common copper pieces of Ananta Deva, each weighing about 80 grains, which in Akbar's time were reckoned as quarter *dâms,* or 40×4=160 to the rupee. The price would therefore be 43,750 rupees for 70 lakhs.

The common weight of India, the *seer* or *setaka,* is now always reckoned at so many *tolas,* or rupees of one tola each, the usual number being 80 tolas. But the very name of *setaka,* or *sat-takâ*=100 *takâs,* and the divisional part of *chha-tâka,* or 6 *tâkas,* show that the weights were originally raised from the old *tangka* or *taka* of 144 grains. This was also the weight of the gold *suvarṇa;* but as the requisite number of copper coins was more readily available, the copper *tangkas* were generally used. In common use at present the seer is reckoned at 80 rupees of 180 grains, thus:—

	No.	Grains.		
Rupees of 180 grains ×	80	=14,400	=1 seer	= 2 lbs. avoir.
Tangkas of 144 grains ×	100	=14,400	=1 setaka	+400 grains.

1 chhetak=14,400÷16=900 grains.

or taking the Tola or Rupee of Delhi at 175 grains.

1 seer = 100 tolas × 175 grains = 14,000 grains = 2 lbs. avoir.
1 chhetak = 14,000 ÷ 16 = 895 grains.

But with a seer of 100 tâkas, the *chha-tâka* would be more exactly $16\frac{1}{6}$, or 16·166 parts—with the heavier tâka of 144 grains, 40 would be exactly equal to one pound Troy—with the lighter tâka of 140 grains, the seer is exactly equal to 2 lbs. avoirdupois.

THE TALENTS OF THE ANCIENT WORLD.

It has been generally considered that in ancient times, the money talent of the *East* was a fixed *weight* which could be applied equally to both gold and silver. In several instances, where actual weighment is mentioned, this very common opinion was no doubt true. But the general adoption of the opinion that a talent of gold must necessarily be a talent *weight* of gold has led many writers, and more especially Biblical writers, into the most monstrous absurdities. According to my judgment, when a talent is named without any notice of its weight, it must be taken simply as a *value* in gold of a talent weight of silver, just as in England a pound is a piece of gold equal in value to the original pound Troy of silver. Thus, the silver penny of William the Conqueror weighs 24 grains, and 20 pennyweights make one ounce, and 12 ounces, or 5,760 grains, make one pound Troy. In dealing with the Attic talent, this principle was always acknowledged; and in Greece, a money talent was a value of the same amount whether in gold or silver.

In ancient Persia, as we learn from Xenophon, a talent of gold consisted of 300 Darics, that is an amount of gold equal in value to a talent weight of silver, which we know consisted of 6,000 silver sigli. As each siglos weighed, according to Mr. Head's valuation, 86·45 grains, the Persian talent contained 518,700 grains, or 71·1 lb. avoirdupois. Now, as we know that the Daric was equal to 20 silver sigli, its actual weight may be obtained by multiplying the weight of the siglos by 20, and then dividing the product by 13, the rate recorded by Herodotus. Thus, 86·45 × 20 = 1729, which divided by 13 gives exactly 133 grains for the weight of the gold Daric.

By applying the same method to the gold talents of the Hebrews, some very curious comparisons may be made with the results arrived at by Biblical writers. The true weight of the talent is most readily obtained from the amount of 100 talents+1775 shekels of silver as the poll tax of a bekah or ½ shekel for each of the persons numbered,[19] thus:—

People numbered	603,550	= bekahs or ½ shekels
2		
	301,775	= full shekels
deduct	1,775	shekels
	300,000	shekels
divided by talents 100 gives	3,000	shekels = 1 talent.

As each Hebrew or Phœnician shekel was 224 grains in weight, the talent was 224×3,000=672,000 grains, or 96 lbs. avoirdupois exactly. That the talent was a heavy one we learn from the story of Naaman and Gehazi, the servant of Elisha.[20] The Syrian lord gave Gehazi two talents of *silver* which were put in two bags, and laid upon two servants. Each servant therefore carried a weight of 96 lbs., or one talent of silver.

But what are we to say about the crown of the king of Rabbah? Joab took the crown of the king of Rabbah which was one talent weight of gold off his head, and set it on David's head.[21] The word *weight* must have been introduced here by mistake. The real weight at 12 rates of silver to 1 of gold would have been 8 lbs., quite enough for a head-piece of any kind.

I turn now to Bagster's Bible, where I find the Hebrew

---

19 Exodus xxxviii. 24.
20 2 Kings v. 33.
21 2 Sam. xii. 30; 1 Chron. xx. 2.

weight of 1 talent set down correctly enough as 114 lbs. Troy, equal to nearly 94 lbs. avoirdupois—while the money talent of silver is valued at £342, and that of gold at £5,475, or just 16 times the value of the silver talent.

It will be a sufficient illustration to apply these two values to the amount of treasure collected by David for the building of the Temple.

	Talents.				
1 Chron. xxii. 14.	100,000	gold	at £5,475	=£547·5	millions.
	1,000,000	silver	at £ 342	=£342·0	,,
			Total .	£889·5	,,

According to Napier (Metallurgy of the Bible), David's treasures amounted to £939,929,687. But this estimate must have included David's private treasure. In the corresponding notice of Josephus,[22] both of the numbers are reduced to one-tenth of those in the Hebrew Bible. But there still remains a total of 110,000 talents of both metals, which, according to my calculation of £350 per talent, whether of gold or silver, would give a hoard of £35 millions of silver, and of £3·5 millions of gold, or altogether of £38½ millions. This sum I would divide again by 10 to bring it within a reasonable amount.

According to my view, *silver* was the standard coin of the ancient world both in Europe and Asia; and whenever gold *money* is mentioned, as, for instance, a talent of gold, it simply means a quantity of gold equal in value to a talent weight of silver. I find that the writer of the article "Nummus," in Smith's Dictionary of Antiquities, held the same view as to the origin of the talent weight.[23] He says, "Unless we know anything to the contrary, we assume a talent of money to mean '*a talent's weight*'

---

[22] Antiq. vii. 14, 2.

[23] P. 810*b*.

of the metal which was chiefly used for money, namely, among the Greeks silver; and, conversely, that the weight of the silver coins, which make up the value of a talent, gives us the amount of talent weight."

All the money contracts of Babylonia and Assyria are recorded in *manas* and *shekels* of silver. In Judæa, we have mention of *Kesitahs*, the value of which is not known. But as the LXX. translated the term by "lamb," ἀμνός, it seems to me highly probable that there may have been some confusion with a *mana*, μνᾶ. The word is used only three times, or rather only twice, as Jacob's purchase of the field at Shechem (or Shalem) for 100 Kesitahs is repeated. The mention of one *Kesitah*, translated ἀμνάδα μίαν, as the present made by each of Job's friends to Job,[24] if of silver must almost certainly have been a *mâna*, as even 100 shekels would have gone but a little way in setting him up again. The same may be said of 100 "lambs," which would not in those days have been worth more than 20 shekels of silver.

When a known value of gold is mentioned, as in the case of Achan who secreted 200 shekels of silver and an ingot or bar of gold of 50 shekels weight, we may accept it as a *mâna* of gold, equal to about 12 times its weight in silver. But this ingot of gold was simply bullion, and I think that its weight of 50 shekels offers a fair explanation of the *amnos* or Kesitah, just before mentioned.

All the ancient weights, according to my view, were derived simply from measures of silver. It follows, therefore, that the money equivalents in gold were not talent weights of gold, but were derived from the current market

---

[24] Job xlii. 11.

value of that metal as bullion when compared with silver. In Persia, the rate was 1 gold=13 silver; and, accordingly, a money talent of gold was only one thirteenth of the weight of a talent of silver. The silver talent was a fixed weight, while gold was simply bullion. This, as I believe from my own experience, was always the case in India, a fact which was very soon discovered by Dr. Kelly when he wrote his account of the "Moneys of India." After stating that there was a gold coin called *Mohur*, which generally passed for 16 rupees, he adds (p. 129), "but this proportion varied according to the *market price of gold*, as *silver was the measure of value.*"

The following table gives the weights and values of the principal ancient talents and their divisions. The money values are all calculated at the rate of 5 shillings per Troy ounce of 480 grains of silver.

	TALENT.			MINA.		SHEKEL.	
	£ Sterling.	lbs. avoir.	Grains.	lbs. avoir.	Grains.	No. shekels.	Grains.
ASSYRIA .	496/	136·0	952,000	2·26	15,866	3,600	264·43
BABYLONIA	248/	68·0	476,000	1·13	7,966	3,600	132·76
LYDIA . By Ingots.	487/	133·77	936,390	2·23	15,606	3,600	260·16
LYDIA . Assyrian.	495/	135·8	950,760	2·26	15,846	3,600	264·10
PERSIA . .	270/	74·1	518,700	1·23	8,645	6,000	86·45
PHŒNICIA	87/	24·0	168,000	0·40	2,800	3,000	56·00
JUDÆA . .	350/	96·0	672,000	1·60	11,200	3,000	224·00
							drachmas
ATHENS. At full weight.	210/	57·6	403,200	0·96	6,720	6,000	67·20 134·40
ATHENS. By good coins.	207·28	56·85	397,980	0·95	6,630	6,000	66·33
CORINTH At full weight.	the	same	as	Ath	ens.		67·20 134·40
CORINTH By good coins.	207·48	56·91	398,340	0·96	6,689	3,000 6,000	132·78 66·89

I have given two slightly different values for the Attic talent, the first according to the hypothetical value assigned to it by most writers on its assumed *full* value, the other according to the average of all the tetradrachms in the Hunter and Leake collections above 264 grains. I have done this for comparison with the Corinthian money, which has been unduly depreciated by modern writers who have fixed an empirical value of the Corinthian Stater at "*about* 130 grains." The average of 36 Corinthian staters in the Hunter and Leake collections is 132·78 grains, giving a drachm of 66·89 grains, which is a little above the Attic drachm.

The Gandharian Alphabet.

Throughout this work I have adopted the name of *Gandharian* for the native characters which were used on all the coins of the Greek kings of India from the time of Demetrius and Eukratides down to the close of their rule under Hermæus. It is often called the *Bactrian* character. But it is very certain that not a single example of this writing has yet been found to the north of the Hindu-Kush. Its use was confined to Ariana on the west of the Indus, and to the Panjâb on the east. Lassen called it *Kabulian*, and Wilson called it *Arianian*. But both of these terms would restrict its use to the west of the Indus, whereas it is found in all the inscriptions discovered at Taxila and Manikyâla, including the version of Asoka's edicts at Mansera to the north of Taxila. M. Senart has called it the "Western Alphabet," meaning, of course, with reference to India. But as it was also used in Kabul and Kandahar, I prefer to call it the *Gandharian* alphabet, as more exactly defining its limits.

The same characters were also used on the coins of the *Kunindas,* whose territory embraced both banks of the Satlej. The *Kunindas,* or *Kulindas,* still exist as *Kunets,* and form nearly two-thirds of the population of the Simla hills. Ptolemy calls the province *Kulindrine,* and the district of *Kulu* now preserves the old name.

The earliest-known examples of its use are the edicts of Asoka at Shâhbâzgarhi to the west, and at Mânsera to the east of the Indus, in B.C. 250. In the eastern Panjâb also most of the native coins bear double legends, one in Gandharian letters, and the other in Indian letters. Many specimens of these coins will be found in Plate IV. There can be no doubt, therefore, that the *Gandharian* alphabet was used throughout the Panjâb, and even to the east of the Satlej, as shown by the copper plate inscription of Kanishka extracted from a Stûpa, 40 miles to the south of Bahâwalpur.

That the Western Panjâb was originally included in Gândhâra we learn from the Mahâbhârata, which states that the two sons of Bharata, named *Pushkara* and *Taksha,* divided Gândhâra between them, and gave their names respectively to *Pushkaravati,* or Peukelaotis, and to *Takshasila* or Taxila. The southern district of Multân must also have been included in Gândhâra, as Al Biruni quoting Utpala, who was a Kashmiri, states that Multân was originally called *Kasyapapura.* Now we know from Hekatæus that *Kaspapuros* was in *Gandarike,* and from Herodotus we learn that it was in Paktuika. Hence it follows that *Gândhára* must have included both Afghanistan and the Panjâb. In fact Kanishka, who lived at Peshâwar in the summer, and at *Chinepati* (near Amritsar) in the winter, is called by the Chinese "King of Gândhâra.

In his work on "The Alphabet," Dr. Isaac Taylor has treated the origin of this alphabet in considerable detail. His conclusion is that it must have been introduced into India "considerably earlier than the reign of Asoka". [II. 259], as at its first appearance it is "in a greatly expanded form, the twenty-two Aramean consonants having been developed into an elaborate alphabet of, at least, thirty-five letters," of which the five vowels, the cerebral letters and several aspirated letters were unknown in the original Aramean alphabet. As I have already noted, these additions must have been made when this alphabet came in contact with the more fully developed alphabet of India.

Exactly the same process took place when the Indian alphabet was introduced into Tibet in the seventh century, A.D., for the cerebrals and aspirates not being required for the Tibetan language, were rejected. Afterwards with the spread of Buddhism, when the cerebral and omitted aspirates were required for the full expression of Indian names and terms, the five cerebral letters were formed by simply revising the dentals, while the aspirates *gh*, *dh*, and *bh* were formed by adding *h* to the letters *g*, *d*, and *b*. Dr. Taylor thinks that the original Aramean alphabet was introduced into Afghanistan and the Panjâb after the accession of Darius, about B.C. 500. I am willing to accept this date, and to place the expansion of the alphabet, with its simple vowel system and aspirates, at about 400 B.C., after its contact with the more fully developed system of the Indian alphabet.

In this Gandharian alphabet, as thus enlarged, the vowel system was very simple. A single character, a pot-hook, like the curved top of a bishop's crozier, was the letter *a*, when initial. The other vowels, when initial, were formed by the simple process of adding side strokes to the *a*, so as to represent *i*, *u*, *e*, and *o*. The same side strokes were attached to the consonants to represent the same vowels in the middle of words. There was only one set of vowels, as no special marks have yet been found to distinguish long and short vowels. As this scheme of attached vowel marks differs only from the more complete system of the Indian alphabet of Asoka in the omission of the short vowels, I conclude that it must have been derived from India. It was certainly not derived from any Aramean source, as all the Aramean alphabets are utterly deficient in the representation of vowels. If speech was given to man to enable him to conceal his thoughts, it seems equally true that all the Aramean alphabets were invented to conceal his written thoughts. I may instance the name of one of the Mahommedan kings of Delhi, which on all his coins is spelt simply *Blbn*. Colonel Dow reads it as *Balin*, and General Briggs as *Balban*. The latter form has been generally accepted, but in an inscription which I found at Gaya, written in Indian characters, which preserve the short vowels, the name is distinctly spelt *Bilbun*.

Dr. Taylor, after discussing the different names that have been proposed for this alphabet by other writers, comes to the conclusion that "on the whole the name *Indo-Bactrian* seems less open to objection than any other." The name of *Bactrian*, which was suggested by Mr. Thomas, "takes no account," he says, "that this alphabet was not only the alphabet of Bactria, but still more emphatically that of *Afghanistan* and the *Panjâb*, whence its chief monuments have been obtained." (II. 258).

I object most emphatically to the propriety of this

name of *Indo-Bactrian*, for the simple reason that not a single inscription in this alphabet has yet been found to the north of the Hindu Kush, or Indian Caucasus. The native legends on the barbarous coins of Antiochus, Euthydemus and Hyrkodes are all expressed in a different form of Iranian characters, which has been called Chaldæo-Pahlavi. They agree in many of the letters with the legends on the Satrap coins of the Akhæmenian kings of Persia, and with those on the coins and the seal-ring of Phrataphernes, Satrap of Hyrkania in the time of Alexander. Most of the letters also agree with those of the Arsakidan and Sassanian coin legends and inscriptions. I refer specially to the coins of the Arsakidans Mithridates and Volagasas, and of the Sassanians Artaxerxes, Sapor and Varoranes, and also to the inscriptions of Hajiâbâd. But this alphabet, which was certainly used in Bactria, and in all the provinces of the Persian and Parthian empires to the north and to the west of Ariana or Afghanistan, has not much in common with the more extensive and more elaborate Gandharian alphabet. The use of the Gandharian alphabet is confined to the south of the Indian Caucasus, where it is found in the Asoka inscriptions at Shâhbâzgarhi and Mânsera, and on all the coins of the Greek kings of Ariana and India. The name of *Indo-Bactrian* is, therefore, both misleading and improper.

In the Indo-Greek series the square copper coins of Demetrius give the earliest coin legends that have yet been found in Gandharian letters. But the fact that the language of the inscriptions, with the pure Indian titles of *Mahârâja* and *Aparajita*, is Indian and not Bactrian, is sufficient to set aside the Bactrian claims. The quarter circle copper pieces of Agathokles, which are of about the same age, spell the king's name in Gandharian letters as *Akathukreasa,* while the Indian legends give *Agathukleasa.* I note the same change of *k* for *g* in some of the early coins of Taxila, which have *Negamâ* in India characters and *Nekama* in Gandharian characters. [See Plate III.]

As all the inscriptions in the Gandharian or Eastern Iranian characters are in the Indian language, so all those in the Chaldæo-Pahlavi or Western Iranian characters are expressed in the Iranian court language of the Arsakian and Sassanian kings. On these latter we find *malkâ* and *malkân-malkâ* instead of the Indian *mahârâja* and *râjâdirâja.* It is admitted that both of these alphabets, which might, perhaps, be called the *Medo-Iranian* and the *Indo-Iranian,* were derived from an Aramean source, but the Eastern alphabet has been so much modified by contact with the more complete and elaborate system of India, that it shows much less distinct traces of its origin than the Western alphabet. I believe that the two forms were originally one alphabet, which was in general use in the time of Darius throughout the Persian empire from the shores of the Ægean Sea to the Eastern limits of the Panjâb.

As the Gâthas, or Hymns of the Avesta, are considered by all Zoroastrians to have been composed by Zoroaster himself, they must have been committed to writing in some cursive form as early as the time of Darius Hystaspes.[25] A script named *Kharosti,* which was read from right to left, is said to have been one of the forms taught to the youthful Buddha. As the name was derived from the inventor of the writing, I think it probable that the name of Zoroaster, or *Zardusht* himself, may have been

---

[25] *Haug's Essays on the Parsis,* by West, pp. 141—257.

preserved in the term *Kharosti*, as the inventor or introducer of that particular form of writing. The *Kharosti* alphabet, under this view of its origin, would naturally have penetrated into every country under Akhæmenian rule. In the provinces directly subject to Persian influence it would have remained almost unchanged; but in the provinces bordering on India, that is throughout Ariana, where the Indian language prevailed, the alphabet was no doubt modified and enlarged to suit the requirements of Indian speech.

The earliest examples of the Gandharian alphabet that have yet been found are the edicts of Asoka at Shâhbâzgarhi to the west, and at Mânsera to the east of the Indus. These may be dated about B.C. 250. The copper coins of Demetrius and Agathokles, B.C. 200, have legends in the same characters. Dr. Taylor places the disuse of the alphabet at the end of the first century, A.D. [II. 259], but he has overlooked the fact that there is a long inscription of Huvishka, the successor of Kanishka, on the Wardak vase, which is dated in the year 51, or A.D. 129, counting from 78 A.D. But the character was in use still later, as there is a short inscription dated in S. 68 from Fatahjang, another dated in S. 84 from Hashtnagar, and a third from Panjtâr, dated in S. 122, or A.D. 200, which I published in 1854. But as there are no inscriptions of Vasu Deva in this character, it seems probable that its decline had already begun in the latter half of the second century A.D. All the known coins which can be attributed to the third century bear corrupt Greek legends with some Indian letters in the field.

The Indian Alphabet.

The Indian Alphabet was in use throughout Northern India at the same time as the Gandharian alphabet. The earliest known examples of both alphabets are the inscriptions of Asoka and the coins of Agathokles. The Pillar inscriptions of Asoka show a highly developed scheme, in which all the long and short vowels are complete. All the letters are reduced to the simplest rigid forms, composed of straight lines and portions of circles. The words also are separated from each other.

As early as the time of Asoka this alphabet had already been arranged in the form that is still in use, in which the consonants are divided into seven groups according to their respective sounds. The seven divisions comprise: 1. Gutturals; 2. Palatals; 3. Cerebrals; 4. Dentals; 5. Labials; 6. Semi-vowels; 7. Sibilants. This arrangement is attributed to Pânini, shortly before the time of Alexander. The proof of the fact was discovered by myself in the arrangement of the pillar-bases of Buddha's canopied walk on the north side of Asoka's temple at Buddha Gaya. The canopy which covered the long-terraced platform was found to have been supported on two rows of pillars, eleven pillars in each row. The bases of the pillars, which are still in situ, were marked in regular succession with vowels in the south row, and with eleven consonants in the north row, all of the Asoka alphabet. It is therefore certain that this highly elaborate alphabet must have been in use for a long time prior to the reign of Asoka. Perhaps B.C. 600 may be accepted as the most probable date of its original formation.

The origin of the Indian alphabet is still unsettled. According to Lassen, Dowson, Thomas, and myself, its origin was indigenous, that is, it was invented by the people of India. But continental scholars are generally in favour of its derivation from some unknown Western source. The latest theory, which has found a strong advocate in Dr. Isaac Taylor (Alphabet I., 314), traces its source to a "South Semitic alphabet," which is supposed to have been the "ancient alphabet of Arabia Felix." I say *supposed* because no proof has yet been offered that the *Sabean* alphabet of South Arabia was in use earlier than the beginning of the second century B.C. This same objection has also been urged by Prof. Max Müller, that "there are no inscriptions from Arabia of a date so early as to be the prototypes of the Indian letters." To this objection Dr. Taylor can only reply, that "there is no reason why the prototype should not be *ultimately discovered* in the unexplored region of Oman, or in some other centre of primitive commerce on the shores of the Persian Gulf." I confess that the probability of future discovery seems to be exactly the other way, and that time will reveal some earlier examples of Indian inscriptions. This seems to be the more likely, as Dr. Taylor himself admits that the Indian alphabet of Asoka was already in existence long before the time of Asoka.

Dr. Taylor then proceeds to some details when he says (p. 523), "of the forty-two Indian letters, the parentage of about *four-fifths* can be assigned with *reasonable certainty*," while there is "no character to which a *plausible* South Semitic parentage cannot be attributed." Dr. Taylor further quotes the letter *J* on the bilingual coins of Agathokles as the representative of a Greek *sigma*. Hence he sees no phonetic difficulty in referring this letter and its derivative, *Sh*, to the Sabean Σ. The example is unfortunate, as the letter *J* on the bilingual coins of Agathokles has a very different form, ☾, which has no resemblance to a Greek Σ. On examining the Sabean alphabet of twenty-two characters, I can find only one letter *B*, which offers a *certain* resemblance to an Asoka letter, namely, *B*, which is a perfect square in both alphabets. Amongst the remaining twenty-one letters I can find only one, namely, *M*, which offers a *plausible* resemblance to the same Indian letter.

But even if there was a general similitude of the letters of the two alphabets, I should rather conclude that the Sabean had been derived from the Indian. It is admitted that the Sabeans were great traders, and that through them the products of India reached Alexandria, but there is no proof that they traded direct with India. On the contrary, it seems more probable that the Indian goods were conveyed to the Persian Gulf, and to the coast of Arabia, as far as Aden, by Indian vessels. In the *Baveru Jâtaka*, *Babylon Jâtaka*, we have an account of some Indian sea-merchants, who carried a peacock for sale to the "land of Baveru."[26] In the Persian cuneiform edicts of Darius, *Babylonia* is called *Babiru*. From these Indian merchants the Sabeans might have derived their alphabet.

That the ancient Indians could make long coasting voyages by sea, we learn from the fact of the Indian conquest and occupation of Java, as far to the East as Babylonia is to the West of India. This conquest was shortly followed by the introduction of the alphabet and religion of India, the monuments of which still remain in the inscriptions and sculptures of Java. What the Indians are known to have done in the East, they may be presumed to have done in the West. If they could plant their alphabet in Java or *Yava-dwîpa*, 1,600 miles to the East of

---

[26] Prof. Rhys Davids, in *Babylonian and Oriental Record*, iv. 7.

the mouths of the Ganges, they may have done the same in Sabea, about 1,600 miles to the West of the mouths of the Indus.

It seems not improbable that this old Indian alphabet, when it was first framed or adopted, did not possess any of the cerebral letters. But their want must have been felt very early to meet the requirements of aboriginal words. Such words as *vaṭa*, the *Baṛ* or Banian tree, and *Khaḍga (Kharg)* the Rhinoceros, would seem to show that the cerebral letters *ṭ* and *ḍ* were additions to the original alphabet to differentiate the sounds of these letters in indigenous words. In the Eastern inscription of Asoka there is only ono sibilant, as in the word *sususa*, which in the Western texts of Gândhâra and Mânsera is written with all three sibilants as *suṣrusha*.[27] It is quite possible, however, that these sibilants actually existed in the alphabet, but were not used, because not required, in the Indian Pali texts. The palatal *ṣ* is, however, found at Kâlsi. But whatever may have been the source of the consonants, it is quite certain that the Indian system of vowels was indigenous.

The Indian alphabet of Asoka is used on the Greek coins of Pantaleon and Agathokles, on several of the early native coins of Taxila, and on all the native inscribed coins from the Indus to the Ganges. M. Senart calls it simply the "Indian alphabet," while Dr. Isaac Taylor prefers the name of the "Asoka alphabet," which I also prefer, as it certifies the date of tho alphabet. Mr. Thomas, and, I believe, also Dr. Burnell, named it the "South Asoka," from some unfounded idea that it was originally framed in Southern India. But, so far as I am aware, not a single

---

[27] Shâhbâzgarhi text; Edict xi., line 23.

inscription in the true Asoka character has yet been found in Southern India. One version of the Asoka Edicts exists at Girnar, in West India, and other versions at Dhaulagiri and Ganjam, in East India. Some short inscriptions have also been found in Ceylon, but they were carried there direct by Asoka's son, Mahindo, who reached the island by sea, from the port of Charitrapura, in Orissa.

Coins of Ancient India.

The earliest Indian coins are small flat pieces of silver, either square or round, adjusted to a certain fixed weight of somewhat more than fifty-six grains, named *Kârsha.* The coin itself was called *Kârshâpaṇa,* from *Kârsha,* the weight, and *âpaṇa,* custom, use. As *Kârsha* also means "a market," the full name is equivalent to the "Kârsha of commerce," or of "common use," or in other words the "current Kârsha." But the Sanskrit form of *Kârshâpaṇa,* which has been preserved in the κορσίπιον of Hesychius, was usually shortened to the Pâli *Kâhâpaṇa* which is the general name found in the Buddhist scriptures, as well as in the cave inscriptions of Western India. But in common use it was still further shortened to *Kâhan,* and in this form it has survived in Bengal until the present day. These silver punch-marked coins are found all over India, from Kabul to the mouth of the Ganges, and from the Himalaya Mountains to Cape Comorin. There were 200 specimens in the South Indian collection of Mackenzie, 500 in Masson's Kabul collection, 373 in Stacy's North Indian collection, 227 in the British Museum. About 2,000 have passed through my hands, and altogether I have seen between 4,000 and 5,000 specimens.

The value assigned to the *Kârshâpaṇa* in the ancient

law-books agrees exactly with that of the *Kâhan* of the present day. The ancient *Kâhâpana* was valued at 16 *paṇas* of *Kauris* (cowree shells), each *paṇa* being equal to 80 cowrees or the same number of *raktikas* or *ratis* of copper. The present *Kâhan* contains 16 *păns*, each of 80 cowrees. From these data we can readily ascertain the value of the copper *paṇas* and the silver *Kârshâpaṇa* with their subdivisions.

The mode of fabrication is evident at once from an inspection of the coins. A piece of silver was first beaten out into a flat plate of about the thickness of a shilling, or somewhat thicker in later times. Narrow strips of about half an inch or more in width were then cut off. Each strip was then cut into separate pieces of the same weight, of about 56 grains, and a final adjustment of the weight was made by cutting small bits off one or more corners of the heavier blanks. The marks of the chisel still remain on the edges of the thicker pieces, which were broken off when the cut did not go clean through the strip of metal. The earliest specimens are generally thin and broad, and of irregular shape. Some are oblong, and some are nearly round; but all are light in weight, and are usually very much worn.

How old these punched-marked coins may be it is difficult to say. They were certainly current in the time of Buddha, that is, in the sixth century B.C. But I see no difficulty in thinking that they might mount as high as 1,000 B.C. They certainly belong to the very infancy of coinage. The only money that could have preceded them would have been blank pieces of silver, which were weighed out, just as Abraham weighed out to Ephron the Hittite 400 shekels of silver, current with the merchant, as the price of the cave of Machpelah.

In a former work I have given all the data in detail from which I determined the weight of the Indian *rati*, or red seed of the *Abrus precatorius* or "wild liquorice." The full weight I found to be 1·83 grains. The *Mâsha* (or "bean"), of 8 ratis, would therefore be 14·64 grains, and the *Kârshâpaṇa* of 4 mâshas would be 58·56 grains. But none of the coins reach this full weight. During my career, I have examined more than 2,000 of these silver pieces. The 20 best specimens of my collection averaged just 55 grains, the heaviest only reaching 56·5 grains. But by far the greater number of these punch-marked coins are so very much worn that the averages obtained by Sir Walter Elliot, 47·10; by Mr. Thomas, 47·69; and by myself, 47·82, from upwards of 800 coins, show how very long they must have been in circulation. I possess one coin which is so much worn as to weigh only 34 grains. But as my 20 best coins give an average of 55 grains, while 10 average 55·6 grains, and one reaches 56·5 grains, I have no hesitation in fixing the original mint issue of these pieces at somewhat more than 56 grains, or say 57·6 grains, which agrees exactly with 32 rati seeds of 1·8 grains each. I adopt these figures on account of their convenience, as the smaller figure is a finite fraction, while the *pala* or *nishka* of 576 grains becomes exactly one-tenth of a Troy pound of 5,760 grains. The gold *suvarṇa* and the copper *paṇa*, with their divisions, are also whole numbers.

The weights of most of the Hindu coins, as given by Manu [Code, viii.—131-32, &c.], are all raised from the seeds of plants, which still exist for approximate verification. These are:—

I. The red-and-black berry of the *Gunja* plant (*Abrus precatorius*, or wild liquorice), which is usually called *Rati* or *Raktika*, the "Red," but is also known as the *Krishnala*, or the "Black," from a black spot at one end. Its weight, as determined by myself by many weighments of thousands of seeds from all parts of India, is 1·8 grain.

II. The seed of the *Mâsha* (the big bean or *Phaseolus*), whose weight is usually accepted as equal to 8 *Ratis*, or 14·4 grains. There are, also, small *Mâshakas* of 2, 3, and 5 ratis each.

III. The seed of the Belleric Myrobolan (*Terminalia Bellerica*), known as *âmalaka* or *Karsha-phala*, that is the "Karsha-fruit," which reaches up to 140 grains in weight, being that of the copper *Kârshâpana*.

COPPER.—The unit of the old copper-money was the *paṇa*, or *Kârshâpaṇa*, which, according to Manu, was equal to one *Kârsha*, or 80 raktikas of copper in weight.[28] The derivation given for the name is from *Kârsha*, the weight, and *âpaṇa*, "custom or use," that is, the "current Kârsha." In Bengal, however, where the name still exists, the *paṇa* (vulgo *pun*), is believed to mean "a handful" of cowrees from *pâṇi* "the hand." This derivation is plausible, as the *paṇa* is usually valued at 20 *gandas* or 80 cowrees, which actually form a very good average handful.

The divisions of the *paṇa* referred to in the Law Books are $\frac{1}{2}$, $\frac{1}{4}$, $\frac{1}{8}$, which are assigned as ferry tolls. The paṇa itself was the usual daily wage of the lowest class of servants, in addition to their food. The fines for various offences assume a decimal scale of $1\frac{1}{4}$, $2\frac{1}{2}$, 5, 10, $12\frac{1}{2}$, 25, 50, 100, 200, 250, and 500 paṇas. I possess specimens of the *paṇa*, and its multiples and divisions, varying from $1\frac{3}{4}$ down to $\frac{1}{16}$, or from 250 grains down to 9 grains. But,

[28] Code viii. 136.

perhaps, the lower values were generally paid in cowrees. Some small pieces from Ujain and Eran, in Malwa, are actually less than 4 grains in weight, and were most probably worth only 2 cowree shells each.

The tale of *Copper* coins was, therefore, as follows :—

Cowrees.	Panas.	NAMES.	WEIGHTS.	
			Ratis.	Grains.
5	$\frac{1}{16}$ paṇa	. . . .	5	9
10	$\frac{1}{8}$ paṇa	Ardha-kâkinî	10	18
20	$\frac{1}{4}$ paṇa	Kâkinî, or Voḍri. . . .	20	36
40	$\frac{1}{2}$ paṇa	Ardhapaṇa.	40	72
60	$\frac{3}{4}$ paṇa	. . . .	60	108
80	1 paṇa	PAṆA or KÂRSHÂPAṆA	80	144
100	$1\frac{1}{4}$ paṇa	. . . .	100	180
120	$1\frac{1}{2}$ paṇa	. . . .	120	216
140	$1\frac{3}{4}$ paṇa	. . . .	140	252
160	2 paṇas	Dwi-paṇa	160	288

The old square punch coins of copper, and all the one-die coins from Taxila, are *paṇas.* The latter are very consistent in maintaining a weight of 140 to 144 grains. The square copper coins of Pantaleon and Agathokles, and the contemporary native coins of two dies, are all pieces of $1\frac{1}{4}$ paṇa, weighing about 180 grains. Copper coins of higher values are rare, and so also are the divisions of the paṇa, and more especially the $\frac{1}{4}$ piece or *Kâkinî* to which H. H. Wilson gives the name of *voḍri.* As this coin weighs only 35 grains, the name of *voḍri* is very suggestive of the Scotch "bodle." Is bodle a gipsy word ?

The tale of *silver* coins is limited to three sizes, the *Kârshâpaṇa,* with its half and its quarter. Mention is also made of a silver *ṣatamâna* of one *pala* or 576 grains. As the word means 100 *mânas* or "measures," the single *mâna* must have been a very small piece of 5·76 grains.

This would be a rather light piece of 3 ratis, which is also spoken of as one of the silver *mâshikas*. The name of *pâdika* is also found in the Bombay Cave inscriptions as being one hundredth part of a *suvarṇa*. As the suvarṇa weighed only 144 grains, the *pâdika* would not have been a gold coin. But as the word means "one quarter," the *pâdika* must have the fourth part of the silver *Kârshâpaṇa*, of which 25 went to the *suvarṇa*. Now, the quarter Kârshâpaṇa is the well-known silver *tangka*, of which we possess many specimens. Its normal weight was, therefore, 14·4 grains, or just the same as the Persian Δανάκη, which was one-sixth of the siglos of 86·4 grains. Both name and weight, therefore, correspond with the Indian *tangka*. The *Kârshâpaṇa* was also called *dharana*, probably meaning a handful of 16 copper paṇas, from *dhṛi*, "to hold." But a more common name was *purâṇa*, or "the old," which could only have been imposed upon it *after* the Greek occupation of the Panjâb. Burnouf saw the importance of this name, as he says that "the *Purâṇa* is a piece of money belonging to a system purely Indian, and therefore *anterior* to the system of the Greeks of Bactriana." [29]

The following list gives the names and weights of the ancient silver coins:—

Panas.	Kârshas.	NAMES.	WEIGHTS.	
			Ratis.	Grains.
4	¼	Tangka, or Pâdika	8	14·4
8	½	Kona	16	28·8
16	1	Kârshâpaṇa, Dharaṇa, Purâṇa	32	57·6
160	10	Ṣatamâna or Pala	320	576

[29] Burnouf, *Introduction à l'histoire du Buddhism Indien*, p. 147, note.

The fact that the *ṣatamâna*, or silver *pala*, contains 10 *kârshapaṇa* shows that the silver reckoning was made on a decimal scale.[30] This is still further developed in the gold coins, for as the *suvarṇa* contained 25 silver *kârshas*, the gold *pala* or *nishka* of 4 suvarṇas must have contained 100 silver kârshas. No specimens of the *ṣatamâna* have yet been seen, although it is mentioned by Kâtyâyana, as well as by Manu. The only known silver coins are the *Kârshâpaṇa*, or *Kâhâpaṇa*, with its divisions of one half and one quarter, and a few specimens which must be eighths. All of these are mentioned in the Mahâwânso, where the monks address the people: "Beloved! bestow on the priesthood either a *Kâhâpaṇa*, or half, or a quarter of one, or even the value of a *mâsa*."

The *gold* money of Northern India consisted of the *suvarṇa* and the *nishka*. No specimens of either have yet been found; and it seems probable that the larger piece may have been only an ingot of gold of a fixed weight. In the Satapatha Brâhmana [xii. 7. 3], mention is made of a "*ṣatamâna* of yellow gold," *hiraṇyaṃ suvarṇam ṣatamânam*. But as the *ṣatamâna* was equal to a *pala* in weight, it was only another name for the *nishka*, which is itself mentioned in the Rig Veda, where the Rishi Kâkshivat receives a present of 100 *nishkas*, with 100 horses, and 100 bulls, from Raja Bhâvayavya. In another place [Rig Veda III-474], mention is made of a present of "ten purses" of gold (*daṣa Koṣayīḥ*), given to the Rishi Garga. As *koṣayī* = *koṣa* means a purse or bag, I infer that the gold was in the shape of dust, and not a coin, nor even an unstamped ingot. We know that the tribute of the Indian Satrapy

---

[30] It is curious that the English troy pound is exactly 10 palas in weight, or 5,760 grains.

was paid to Darius in "gold dust" (Herod. III. 94). We know, also, that even at the present day small amounts of gold dust, of the fixed value of 8 rupees, tied up in pieces of cloth, circulate freely in the Himalayan provinces. But the Indian gold was also made into *pindân*, or "ingots," which, probably, were known to the Hebrews (Isaiah xiii. 10), as the "golden wedge, or tongue of Ophir." An earlier mention of the "golden ingot of 50 shekels weight" is found in the story of Achan. Now, fifty Hebrew shekels weight of gold would be exactly equal to 20 *palas*, or *nishkas* or *şatamânas*, a fact which goes far to prove that Ophir, or Σωφίρ, was part of India.

Although no specimens of ancient Indian gold money have come down to us, yet we know, from the Erythræan Periplus, that on the Eastern coast there was a native gold coin called *Kaltis*, from which the merchants derived a profit by giving Roman gold and silver money in exchange. The name seems to be the same as the *Kalutti* of Malayâlam, the *Karanda* of Ceylon, and the *Kalanju* of South India.[31] The seed is used as a weight, which is now over 50 grains. Taking this weight as a guide, I have little hesitation in identifying the *Kaltis* with the gold *Hûn* of South India, which averages about 52 grains. The oldest gold coins noted by Sir Walter Elliot are quite plain and smooth.[32] "They weigh about 52 grains, evidently derived from the *Kalanju*, their original name being *pon*, which simply means gold in Tamil, becoming *hon* in Kanarese, and the origin of the Mohammedan *hûn*." I must confess, however, that I have always looked upon

[31] Walter Elliot, *Coins of S. India*, p. 48.
[32] W. Elliot, p. 53.

hon and *hûn* as being the same as *soṇ*, which is the spoken form of *suvarṇa*, "gold." The coin itself is called *Hûna* in the Nasik inscription, No. 5 of Stevenson (Bombay Pl. V).

With reference to the absolute non-existence of any very old Indian gold coins, my explanation is a very simple one. During the early centuries of the Christian era, the Roman trade with India increased to such an extent that the annual balance in favour of India amounted to nearly half a million pounds sterling. This was made good by sending actual cash, both in gold and silver to India. Pliny's words are "minimâque computatione millia sestertium annis omnibus India et Seres peninsulaque (Arabia) imperis nostro adimant."[33] "At the lowest reckoning one hundred million sesterces (about £800,000) are taken from us every year by India, the Seres, and Arabia." Gibbon (c. 2), reckons the amount as "upwards of £800,000;" and in a note he adds, "in another place Pliny gives half that sum, quingenties H.S. for India, exclusive of Arabia." What became of this great influx of gold? My explanation is that in North India it was received by the Indo-Scythian Kushân Princes, Wema Kadphises, Kanishka, Huvishka, and Vâsudeva, whose gold coinage is now found in such large quantities. Their gold coins are of the same weight as those of the early Cæsars. In South India the gold coin circulated just as it came, which satisfactorily accounts for the frequent finds of Roman gold coins at the present day, and the total absence of any early Indian gold coins.

In North India the great Gupta kings introduced their own coinage, while they still adhered to the Roman

---

[33] *Hist. Nat.*, xii. 41 (18).

standard and the Indo-Scythian types. In South India, however, there appeared the new gold coins called Hûns, which would seem to have been intended for half-dinârs of the Roman standard. At a later date in North India a few Hindu chiefs issued gold coins, which, being heavier than the Hûns, were perhaps intended for half suvarnas. But the issue was chiefly confined to the Chandel Rajas of Mahoba, and the Rathor Rajas of Kanauj.

The gold coins of South India, the *Hûn* and its subdivisions, are very numerous. I take the *Hûn* to be the original "gold *Kârsha,*" of 57·6 grains, which has now dwindled down to 52 and 53 grains. I find that 10 of the old Hûns, published by Walter Elliot, give an average of 55 grains, while the gold *fanams*, or "tenths," average 5·75 grains. A few still older pieces, which range from 63 to 66·4 grains, give an average of 64·9 grains. But these are, perhaps, half-suvarnas, of 72 grains, full weight. The oldest of them are broad, thin, punch-marked coins, of more than 66 grains. They bear the names of Châlukya, and are assigned by W. Elliot to the fifth and sixth centuries A.D. I acquiesce in this date, as the inscribed silver coins that were found in their company are of about the same period.

The actual age of the heavier Hûns, or gold Kârshas, is not known; but I am able to fix the date of one of the most remarkable specimens as certainly not later than the eleventh century. In the history of Kashmir it is stated that Raja Harsha Deva "liked the customs of the south, and introduced coins like those current in Karnâta."[34] Now I possess a gold coin of this king, with the name

---

[34] Raja Tarangini, B. vii. (*Translation by Jogesh Chunder Dutt*, p. 238).

of "Sri Hársha Deva" on one side, and on the other a caparisoned elephant walking to the right, which is an evident copy of one of the Karnâta gold coins of the same type. [See W. Elliot's Coins of South India, Plate III., 109; and Marsden Numismata Orientalia, Plate XLVIII., 1059.] But the Kashmir coin is a half *suvarṇa*, of 72 grains, while the southern coin is a *Hûn*, of 58 grains. Harsha Deva reigned from A.D. 1089 to 1101.

The gold coins of ancient India were as follows:—

NAMES.	Grains.
1/10 Hûn, or Fanam	5·28
¼ Hûn, or Mâda	13·20
½ Hûn, or Pratâpa	26·40
1 Hûn [Varâha, or Pagoda]	52·80
1 Kârsha (full weight)	57·60
½ Suvarṇa	72·00
1 Suvarṇa	144·00
1 Nishka, Pala, or Ṣatamâna	576·00

In former days it was the general opinion of classical scholars that the art of coinage had been introduced into India by the Bactrian Greeks.[35] Some twenty years ago I pointed out a passage of Quintus Curtius, which records a gift of eighty talents of *coined silver*, which was made to Alexander himself on his arrival at Taxila by the native Raja of the country. The term used by Curtius is *signati argenti*, which fortunately admits of no other meaning than that of "*coined* silver." I argued also that the types, the shape, and the standard of the earliest Indian money, the square punch-marked silver, and the square one-die copper coins could not have been copied from the Greek money. Since then I have discovered two monumental evidences of the antiquity of these square Indian

---

[35] *Curtius Vit. Alex.*, xviii. 13—41.

coins in the Buddhist sculptures of Mahâbodhi and Bharhut. The former is as old as Asoka himself, B.C. 250, having been executed during his reign; the latter are somewhat later, or about B.C. 150. In both of these there is a representation of the famous story of the Jetavana, or purchase of the garden of Prince Jeta by the merchant, Anâtha. According to the legend the purchaser had to cover the whole surface of the garden with a layer of gold coins. In both sculptures the servants of Anâtha are seen laying the coins, edge to the edge, as the inscription states. As all the pieces are *square*, they clearly represent the punch-marked money that was current in the time of Asoka. I have given representations of both sculptures in the frontispiece.[36] The story will be found in the Appendix.

That the native square copper coins were contemporary with the similar shaped copper coins of Pantaleon and Agathokles was lately proved by the discovery of nine pieces of Pantaleon and fifteen of Agathokles, along with eighty-four native pieces of the single-die, and twenty-seven of the double-die coins.[37] Now, it is remarkable that the single-die coins were all of the indigenous weight of eight *ratis*, or 140 grains, while those of the Greek kings and the double-die native coins were of 100 *ratis*, or 180 grains.

In favour of my arguments to the priority of a native Indian coinage, I pointed to the name of *purâṇa*, or "old," which was applied in the Buddhist *sutras* to the silver punch-marked *Kârshas*. I then asked "under what possible circumstances could the Indian silver

---

[36] Plate A.

[37] See *Archæol. Survey of India*, vol. xiv.

Kârsha have been called 'old' at the time of the compilation of the Buddhist sutras, about 200 B.C.?" I replied that they must have received this name when they came in contact with the Greek money of Alexander's successors. The *round* Greek drachms and hemi-drachms were the *new* silver money, and the *square* native Kârshas were the *old* money, or the *purâṇas*.

My other argument against the Greek origin of the punch-marked coins was, that any Indian coins copied from the Greek money would have been in silver, and of the Greek standard in weight. This argument has been satisfactorily proved by the discovery of the coins of the native princes, Dhâra-Ghosha, Mahâdeva, Rudra-Varma, and Amogha-bhûti of the Greek standard, with inscriptions on both sides. As these coins were found in company with the Greek Philopator hemi-drachms of Apollodotus they must have been current at the same time. But the old punch-marked coins were also current along with them, as a few specimens *much worn* were some years earlier found in company with hemi-drachms of Antimachus II., Philoxenus, Lysias, Antialkidas, and Menander.[38]

North India.—Punch and Cast Coins.

Plate I.

In Plate I., Figs. 1 to 15 are silver *Kârshâpaṇas* or *Purâṇas* from several different places. Figs. 16, 17, 18 are half *Kârshâpaṇas* or *Koṇas*, and Fig. 19 is a quarter *Kârshâpana*, called *Tangka*, and also *Pâdika*. On the earliest specimens, or, perhaps, I should say, on those

---

[38] Sir E. C. Bayley was my authority for this fact.

PLATE I.

N. INDIA

which have been the shortest time in circulation, the punch-marks are confined to one side of the piece. As a general rule the best preserved coins are not much worn, whereas those that are nearly worn smooth betray their long circulation by their light weight. Fig. 15 is a good example of long wear, as it weighs only 34 grains, the original weight having been not less than 56 grains. This coin was found, along with two others weighing 35 and 42 grains, in the deposit at the foot of the Vajrâsan, or throne of Buddha, in the temple of Mahâbodhi, at Buddha Gaya. As this deposit was made about A.D. 150, during the reign of the Indo-Scythian king, Huvishka, we learn that punch-marked coins were still in circulation at that time. The three coins weigh 111 grains, giving an average of only 37 grains. But, as the general average of upwards of 800 of these coins from all parts of India is upwards of 47 grains, I am willing to accept a loss of 19 grains in weight in about 600 years circulation, or, roughly, from B.C. 450 to A.D. 150, as very exceptional. These three coins show a loss of upwards of 3 grains per century, while the average loss of these punch-marked coins was not more than one grain and a half in a century. It must be remembered that they were all hardened with copper alloy.

These punch-marked coins are generally known in South India by the name *Sâlâka*, which is usually applied to a domino, as well as to the oblong die which is used at the game of *pachisi*. I infer that this name has been given them partly on account of their oblong form, and partly on account of the marks upon them. At first the stamps were punched quite clear of each other, and on one side only. But as new stamps were found necessary they were punched over the old ones, until on some pieces it is difficult to trace all the original forms. As a general rule the opposite side was very sparingly stamped, as on No. 10, or sometimes only one stamp was made on the reverse, as on Nos. 12 and 14.

I have often thought that where only one stamp is found on the reverse it might possibly be the peculiar symbol of the place of issue. I found, for instance, that about one-third of the silver punch coins discovered at Taxila bore the same stamp placed alone on the reverse, and as this particular stamp is found as the full reverse of the small gold coins of Taxila, I think that my conjecture may be correct. This peculiar stamp is seen on the reverse of the silver coins 1 and 2 of Plate II., and on the gold coin No. 18, all from Taxila.

A second symbol I have noted as being often placed alone on the punch-marked coins from Benares and the surrounding districts. This is well shown on the reverse of Fig. 14, Plate I. It looks something like a bale of cotton, but I cannot suggest its application to any particular place.

A few of the symbols are no doubt very suggestive, but the most that can be said in their favour is, that they are not impossible. The following are a few of these possibilities:—

1. A *Bull* or *Cow* [Sk. *Vatsa=Vacca*] a very common symbol on the coins of the *Kosâmbi*, the capital of the *Vatsas*, or, as they were also called, the *Vatsa puttriyas*.

2. An *armed soldier* [Sk. *Yoddha*] I would refer to the *Yaudheyas*, who derived their name from *Yuddha*, "battle," as they were renowned as warriors even in the time of Pânini.

3. A Tree, *Udumbara* fig tree (*Ficus glomerata*), on the

coins of the *Odumbaras,* who are also mentioned by Pânini.

4. A *Square Tank,* with or without fish, might be referred to the holy Pushkara or Pokhar, "a tank," near Ajmer, or to the famous city of *Pushkara,* or *Pushkalâvati* (Peukelaotis), near Peshâwur.

5. A *Snake* [Sk. *Ahi*] might refer to the ancient city of *Ahi-chatra,* or *Ahi-Kshetra,* which was famous in both Buddhistical and Brahmanical story.

6. A *Peacock* [Sk. *Mayûra*] might refer to the city of *Mayûrapura,* or "Peacock-town," now *Maya-pura,* near Hardwar. The old town of *Mo-yu-lo,* or *Mayûra,* is described by the Chinese Pilgrim, Hwen Ynsang, as being 20 li., or upwards of three miles in circuit.

7. A *Palm* tree [Sk. *Kharjûra,*] might be referred to the old capital of the Chandels called *Kharjûr-pur.*

8. A *Lotus* flower [Sk. *Padma*], might refer to *Padmâvati,* the old title of the famous fortress of Narwar, the capital of Raja Nala.

9. The *Pâtali,* or Trumpet Flower, might refer to *Pâtaliputra,* or *Pâlibothra,* the capital of the *Mauryas,* on the Ganges.

10. A *Female* figure, standing to front, with five rays ascending from her head. The number five, or *panch,* may, perhaps, refer to *Panchâla,* the capital of Raja Drupada, whose daughter, Draupadi, was married to five husbands, the Pânch Pândava. The figure occurs on several of the actual coins of Panchâla.

Some of the kings also placed on their money punning allusions to their names, thus:

Sûrya Mitra and Bhânu Mitra have each got a representation of the "Sun" [Sk. *Sûrya* and *Bhânu*].

Chandra Gupta has a "Crescent," [Sk. *Chandra*, the Moon].

Kumâra Gupta has a figure of the goddess *Kumâri Devi*.

Raja Hasti has an Elephant [Sk. *Hasti.*]

But amongst all these numerous symbols, I do not find one that points unmistakeably to Brahminism, such as the trident of Siva, or the shell of Vishnu. But I notice several symbols that were certainly Buddhist. Of these, the most remarkable are the *Chaitya* symbol, and the holy Tree, surrounded by a Buddhist railing. The Swastika occurs, but it was common to both religions. The Pentagonal Star is also seen; but both of these symbols have also been found in other countries.

Another explanation of some of these symbols has struck me as possible, or perhaps, even probable. I have a suspicion that several of the symbols may have been the private marks of ancient money-changers. At the present day these men are still in the habit of placing their own particular stamps on the rupees that pass through their hands, so that when any of the coins come back to them again, they know their value without making a second testing. Now, the old money changers might have had symbols referring to their own names, thus: the "Sun," for Sûrya Dâs; a "Snake," for Nâga Sen; and an "Elephant," for Gaj Sinh. Bir Deo might have had a "soldier," Gopâl a Bull, and Khajur Varma a "Palm" tree (*Khajur*). The number of these symbols is so great, nearly three-hundred, that their origin was probably due to several different causes. My friend, Mr. W. Theobald, has been making a complete collection of them, which will shortly be published, with his explanations of most of them.

In Plate I. I have given only a selection of the most striking examples.

The punch-marked COPPER coins are much rarer than the silver coins. At least, one-half of those that I have seen are simple forgeries of the silver coins, which betray themselves by their weight (that of the fifty-grain Kârsha), and sometimes by the silver still adhering to them. The finest copper specimens that I have got all came from Eran, see Plate XI. But in Plate I. I have given four specimens of different weights, three of which are nearly worn smooth. Some of them must be of early date, as the marks are few, and apart from each other, and are confined to one side of the coin.

The following is the scale of the copper coins:—

	Weight.	
⅛ paṇa, or ½ kâkiṇi . . .	10 ratis or	18 grains
¼ paṇa, or 1 kâkiṇi . . .	20 ,,	36 ,,
½ paṇa, or ardha-paṇa . .	40 ,,	72 ,,
1 PAṆA	80 ,,	144 ,,
1¼ paṇa	100 ,,	180 ,,
1½ paṇa	120 ,,	216 ,,
1¾ paṇa	140 ,,	252 ,,
2 paṇas	160 ,,	288 ,,

The four specimens in the Plate are:—

No. 20—weighing	159	grains	a heavy *Paṇa*
No. 21 ,,	250	,,	= 1¾ paṇa
No. 22 ,,	229	,,	= 1½ ,,
No. 23 ,,	79·5	,,	= a heavy ½ paṇa.

The square single-die coins of Taxila are Paṇas of 144-grains. The square double-die coins, and also those of Pantaleon and Agathokles, are pieces of 1¼ paṇa of 180 grains.

The CAST COINS of ancient India are very numerous.

They are all of copper, and, from the scarcity of the copper punch-marked coins, I am led to believe that they must have been current together with the silver coins. Nos. 24 and 25 are double coins, having never been separated since taken from the mould. They show an Elephant and Chaitya, and are found all over North India. No. 26, with a Bull, and No. 27 with a Lion and Flagstaff, are rarely found in the Panjâb. No. 28 is found chiefly about Benares. It is of six different sizes, weighing respectively, 107, 76, 26, and 11 grains. No. 29 shows a Bodhi tree surrounded with a railing. These coins are rather rare. No. 30 was obtained at Kosam, but it shows the six bulls of the Malwa coins from Ujain, Eran and Besnagar. The cast coins are rare at some places, and common at others. There are few cast coins at Taxila, but at Ayodhya all the earliest coins are cast ones.

Coins of Taxila.

Plates II. and III.

Just twenty-five years ago I identified the present *Shâh-dheri* or *Dheri Shâhân*, that is, "the royal residence," with the ancient Taxila. The old fortified city, which is still surrounded by stone walls, is called *Sir-kap*, which all the people agree in stating is only a slight alteration of *Sir-kat*, or the "cut head."[39] Now this is the exact meaning of *Taksha-ṣira* or *Takha-ṣira*, which was the Buddhist form of the name of *Taksha-sila* or *Takha-sila*, from which the Greeks made Taxila. The change of name to *Taksha-sira* was made to suit the legend of Buddha having cut off his head to offer to a hungry tiger.

---

[39] *Archæol. Survey*, xiv. 8.

PLATE II.

TAXILA.

The legend now exists in a changed form, which makes the Raja Sir Kap a gamester, who used to play with strangers for "heads," which he always won by fraud, and immediately cut off.

The coins found on this site are very numerous, beginning with the earliest punch-marked silver pieces, and the square copper pieces of single dies, and of the standard peculiar to India, all of which I take to be anterior to the Greek conquest of Alexander.

Figs. 1 and 2 of Plate II. are silver *kârshas* or *purâṇas*, of the usual punch-marked standard of over 50 grains. On the reverse of both specimens is the peculiar symbol, which I have conjectured to be the mark or sign of Taxila. See also fig. 18, where the same symbol occurs on a gold coin. Here we see the lion, or, perhaps, the tiger of the Buddhist legend, in its earliest form, which was afterwards matured on the square copper pieces of double dies, and on the square pieces of Pantaleon and Agathokles. These small copper coins are common.

Figs. 6 to 17 are single-die coins, the reverse sides being quite plain. They present some well-known Buddhist symbols, such as the Chaitya and the Bodhi tree. The Swastika also is a well-known symbol. On No. 6 I recognize a monolith standing beside the Chaitya. On No. 12 I see the plan of a monastery with its cells, and a stupa in its courtyard. On No. 13 there is a building which may be a temple. On Nos. 9 and 11 there is a pile of bales, which on No. 14 is an object of worship. On No. 17 the symbol commonly called *Chaitya* is the object of worship. The legend on No. 17, in Asoka characters, is *Vataswaka*, of which the meaning is unknown. *Vata* is one of the names of a cowree shell, and as the coin is a *pana* of 145 grains, or 80 shells in value, it may, perhaps, have some reference to the number 80, *asiti*. But *vata* also means "round," and may, therefore, refer to the *shape* of the coin, in which case, *swaka* or *suka* would be the *name* of the piece, "the round *suka*."

No. 15 is a cast coin, weighing 306 grains. It is, therefore, a piece of 2 paṇas, the only one that I have ever seen. Nos. 19 and 20 are double-die coins, with symbols on both sides.

No. 18 is a gold coin, weighing 32·8 grains. It may be either a quarter *suvarṇa*, or a quarter stater.

Nos. 21 and 22 are cast coins, on which a snake is the prominent figure. The legend, in Asoka characters, reads *Kâḍasa*, which may, perhaps, have some reference to the descendants of the serpents called *Kâdru*.

The coins in Plate III. are all double-die pieces. Nos. 1 and 2, with the Elephant and Lion types, have already been referred to. These coins are very common, not only in the Western Punjab, but in the Kabul valley. They average upwards of 180 grains in weight; there are also smaller pieces of the same types, weighing upwards of 100 grains, and others of 68 and 70 grains. A large coin like No. 2 was found in a stûpa at *Ushkar* in Kashmir, opposite Barâhmula. It formed the sole deposit, and was probably placed there during the reign of Asoka.

Figs. 3 and 4 present an Elephant and a galloping Horse. The Horse appears to have been copied from the copper coins of Euthydemus. On No. 4 there is a Greek monogram under the horse, which may form either KA or TA. The latter might refer to Taxila.

Fig. 5 is of rare occurrence. On the obverse, between a Chaitya and a Bodhi tree, is seen an Elephant full front. The two ears are spread out to the right and left of the lobes of the head; the trunk hangs down the middle, with a tusk on each side; while all four legs are displayed, the hind legs appearing outside the fore legs. The symbols require no description. The coins are of two kinds, thick and thin, the former weighing from 114 to 121 grains, the latter only 88 grains.

Fig. 6. The coins of this type are all thin pieces, of three different sizes, the largest weighing 100 grains, the middle sizes ranging from 58 to 64 grains, and the smallest only 27 grains. The Buddhist symbol on the obverse has a small head on the top of the middle limb. It stands on a Buddhist railing, and is flanked by a small *chaitya* symbol on each side.

Fig. 7 is of very rare occurrence. I have only two specimens and there is a third in the British Museum. The weight, 75 grains, is that of a half paṇa. The head, with short ears and protruded tongue, may be that of a *Râkshasa*, or "demon," as an opponent of Buddhism. There are traces of some letters over the head. The reverse is a Buddhist symbol, flanked by a *chaitya* symbol on each side.

We now come to a series of rare inscribed coins, which are found only at Taxila. The legends are in beautifully formed Asoka characters, both Gandharian and Indian. One word occurs on all of them. In Indian letters it is usually written *Negamâ*, a single variant being *Nigama*. In Gandharian letters it is written *Nekama*. I take this to be the name of the piece, whether it be a coin or a weight. *Nigama*, like *νόμος*, means "custom, habit, use;" and *Negamâ*, like *νόμισμα*, I take to be either a coin or weight of fixed value, as ascertained or settled by common use. Over the word Negamâ there is a single stroke or bar, as if to designate *one negamâ*. On the opposite side there is a "steelyard" very clearly represented, over which is the word *dojaka*, in Gandharian letters on some coins, and in Indian letters on other coins. On fig. 8 this word is replaced by *râlimata*, and on fig. 11 by *antarotaka*. On fig. 12 there is only an incomplete word, ending in *ḍare*, in Gandharian characters.

On another class of coins, fig. 13, with a wheel, or *Dharmachakra*, on one side, there is a new legend in Gandharian letters, which I read as *pancha nekamma*, or "Five Nekamas."

The only word now existing which has any resemblance to *negama*, or *nekama*, is *gani*, or *kani*, which, in Kashmir, was the unit from which all the coins were derived. The *Bâragani* was a coin of 12 (or properly of 12½) *ganis*; the *Panchi* was equal to 2 *Bâraganis*, or one "twenty-fiver"; 4 *panchis* made one *hat* (or *sat*) or "hundreder"; and 10 *hats* made one *Sâsnu* (*sahasrânu*) or "thousander."[40] Now the *panchi*, being one-fourth of Akbar's *dâm* of 324 grains, must have weighed 81 grains of copper, which is, in fact, the mean weight of the copper coins of Kashmir. If we take *pancha-negama* as the possible original of *panchi* (or *panchi gani*) then *negama* may be still preserved in *gana* or or *gani*. As three of my coins weigh 236 grains, the *pancha nekama* averages 78·66 grains, the heaviest coin being 82 grains. Taking the true average as 81 grains, the one *negama*, or *nekama*, would have been $\frac{81}{25}$ or 3·24 grains. It seems to me not improbable that the old *negami* may have been preserved in Kashmir as the *gani*.

But, unfortunately, this explanation is of no use with regard to the other names, *Dojaka* and *Râlimata*. Their weight varies from 105 to 120 grains, and their general aspect is so different from that of the other coins that it

---

[40] Gladwin, *Ain Akbar.*, ii. 126.

does not seem possible that they could have been connected. Perhaps the names may be those of places, or even of men, and "Dojaka's Token" and "Râlimata's Token" might be the actual names of the pieces.

No. 14 is a thin coin, weighing only 57 grains. It bears the remains of a long inscription, which unfortunately is not legible.

The variant spellings with *g* and *k*, in *negama* and *nekama*, are common to other names on the Western frontier, as in Agathukliya, and Akathukliya, Gandhâra and Kandahar, and also in Mihir-kul and Mihir-gul. It is curious to find both spellings of *Negama* and *Nekama* in the same inscription in one of the Kânhari caves near Bombay. [Journal of Bombay Asiat. Soc. xii. 407.]

In 1884 a small parcel of 143 square copper coins, of several of the types just described, was found at Shâh-dheri, the ancient Taxila. Of these, 127 specimens came into my possession, and 8 others were sent for my inspection. They comprised the following kinds:—

84 Indian coins of one face only,		average weight,	140·8 grains.
27 Indian coins of two faces		" "	183·3 "
9 coins of Pantaleon	24 Greek	" "	180·5 "
15 coins of Agathokles			

It will be observed that the single-face coins with blank reverse are all of the Indian standard of 80 *ratis*, or 144 grains, while the two-face coins, both Indian and Greek, are the heavier standard of 100 *ratis*, or 180 grains.

As all these coins were found together, they must have been current at the same time. But as the greater number are of the Indian standard, I infer that they must belong to the indigenous coinage prior to the Greek occupation. I infer also that the deposit must have been made at an early period of the Greek rule, as shown by the presence of the coins of the two early Greek Kings, Pantaleon and Agathokles. The Greek coins preserve the Indian type of the Lion, as well as the square shape.

Odumbara.

Plate IV.

The name of *Odumbara*, or Audumbara, is derived from the *Udumbara* fig tree (Ficus glomerata). According to Pânini any country possessing these trees may be called *Audumbara*.[41] There is a country of this name now called Kachh, where Pliny places a people named *Odonbeores*.[42] But all my coins were found in the Northern Panjâb, beyond Lahore, and this I find is the very part of the country where the coins were discovered. Varâha Mihira twice couples the Udumbaras with the *Kapisthalas* ; the Markandeya Purâna does the same, while the Vishnu Purâna couples them with the *Traigarttas* and *Kulindas*. The Kapisthalas are the *Kambistholi* of Arrian, and their name is still preserved in the abbreviated form of *Kaithal* to the south of Ambâla. The Traigarttas are the people of Katoch or Kângra, and the *Kulindas* are the people of Ptolemy's *Kulindrine*, or the districts on both banks of the Satlej, which are now occupied by the *Kunets* of Kullu and Kunâwar. The name of *Kulinda* is also written *Kuninda*, and this form will be found on some of the coins about to be described. The country of the Odumbaras must therefore be looked for near Kângra and the Kunet districts, and there the name still exists in the rich tract between the Râvi and Biâs Rivers, comprising the forts of Pathân-

---

41 Goldstücker, quoted by Hall, *Vishnu Purana*, ii. 188.
42 *Nat. Hist.* vi. § 75.

PLATE IV.

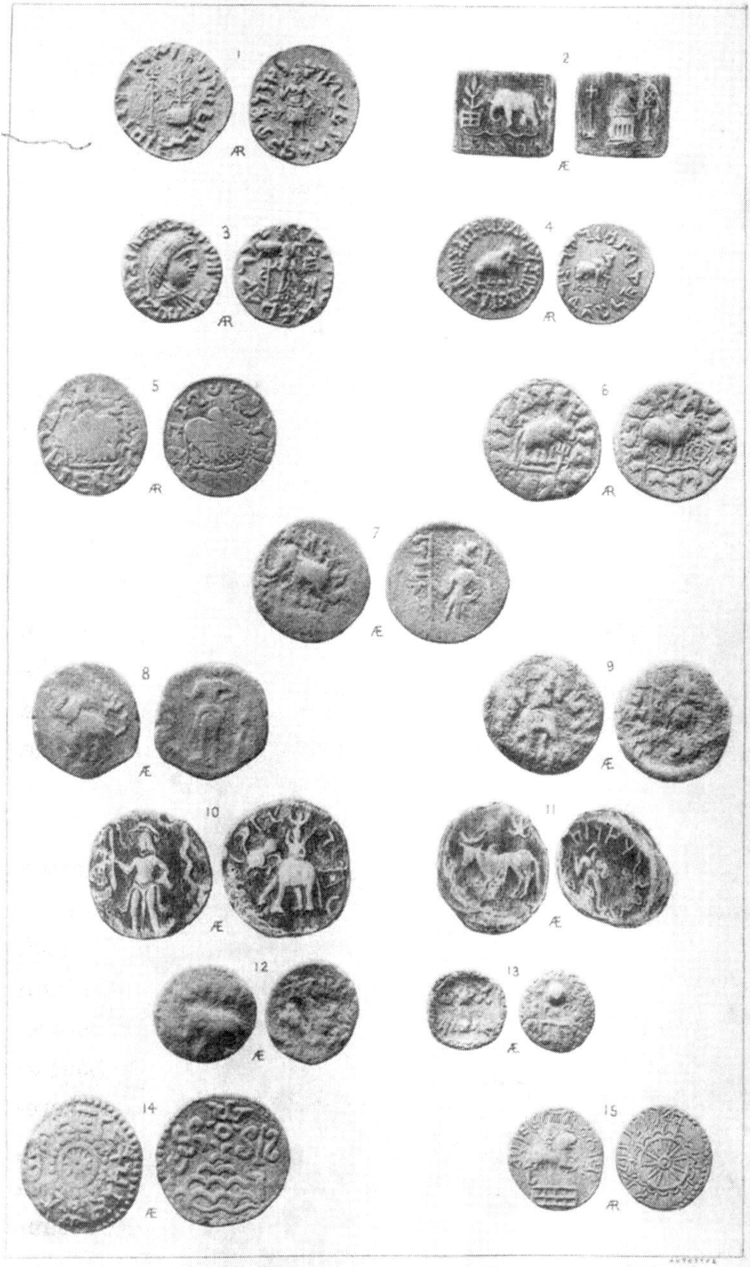

ODUMBARA.

kot and Nûrpur (or *Damari*). The old fort of *Damâla* was captured by Ibrahim Ghaznavi.[43] The town was properly called *Dahmari*, the name of *Nurpur* being that of the fort which was built or repaired by Jahângir, and named after his wife, Nûr Jahân. Reinaud [p. 113] calls Dahmâlah the capital of Jâlandhar. The district itself which gave its title to the Raja, was named *Pathâna*. The name is a Hindu one, being derived from *Paithâna*, the spoken form of *Pratishthâna*, which I would identify with Ptolemy's *Batanagara*.[44]

In A.D. 1573 Chota, a relative of the Raja, held *Damhari* against Akbar's general.

In A.D. 1594 Vasu Deva, Zamindâr (Raja) of Mân and *Pathân*, rebelled against Akbar.

The coins of the *Odumbaras* consist of 2 silver hemi-drachms and 5 small square copper pieces. One of the silver coins, now in the Lahore museum, was found in a field near Jwâla Mukhi, in company with 3 silver pieces of the Kunindas, and 28 Philopator hemi-drachms of Apollodotus. My silver coin was obtained in the Pathânkot district, and my 7 copper coins were all found in Pathânkot itself. As they all bear the name of *Odumbara*, their assignment is quite certain. Their age may also be assigned, with some certainty, to the time of Apollodotus, or about 100 B.C.

Raja DHARA-GHOSHA.

Plate IV., Fig. 1. Æ. 0·7. Weight 37·5 grains. Dupl. Lahore Museum.

Obv.—Siva, standing to front with r. hand raised to head, and leopard's skin over l. arm; similar to figure of Herakles crowning himself. Legend in Arian

---

43 Rashid-ud-din, H. M. Elliot, i. 62.
44 H. M. Elliot, v. 357.

Pali characters. *Mahadevasa rajna Dhara-Ghoshasa Odumbarisa*—across field *Viswamitra.*

Rev.—Tree [*Udumbara* fig-tree (?)] surrounded by Buddhist railing. To left Siva's trident with battle-axe attached. Indian Pali legend, *Mahâdevasa rajna Dhara-Ghoshasa Odumbarisa.*

Plate IV., Fig. 2. Æ. 0·6. Weight 22 to 25 grains. The Indian *Kâkinî.*

Obv.—Elephant before Tree (Udumbara fig-tree) surrounded by Buddhist railing, snake below. Arian legend, incomplete, *Odumbara.* . . .

Rev.—Pointed-roofed temple of two or three storeys, with pillars. *Swastika* to l. on pillar. *Dharma-chakra,* with pendant garlands, to r.

Plate IV., Fig. 3. Ꭱ. Hemi-drachm of Zoïlus from Pathânkot, with trident battle-axe of Siva in field of reverse, to illustrate No. 1.

Plate IV., Fig. 4. Ꭱ. Hemi-drachm of Apollodotus, with Elephant and Bull, to illustrate figs. 5 and 6.

Raja MAHADEVA.

Plate IV., Fig. 5. Ꭱ. 0·65. Weight 33 grains. Author.

Obv.—Elephant with upraised trunk moving to l., towards trident battle-axe of Siva. Indian legend, *Bhâgavata Mahâdevasa Râja-raja.*

Rev.—Humped Indian Bull to r.; lotus flower under head to r. Arian legend, *Bhagavata Mahadevasa Rajarajna.*

Raja RUDRA VARMA.

Plate IV., Fig. 6. Ꭱ. 0·7. Weight ——. Lahore Museum.

Obv.—Elephant with upraised trunk moving to r., towards trident battle-axe of Siva. Indian legend, *Râjna Vamakisa Rudra Varmasa Vijaya.*

Rev.—Humped Indian Bull to r., flower under head. Arian legend, *Rajna Vamakisa Rudra Varmasa Vijayata.*

Raja AJA-MITRA.

Plate IV., Fig. 7. Æ. 0·7. Weight 71 grains. Author.

Obv.—Elephant with upraised trunk moving to l., towards tree in Buddhist railing. Indian legend, (*Rajna*) *Aja Mitasa.*

Rev.—Man standing to l. with spear in r. hand, snake to r. Arian legend, *Rajna Ája Mitàsa.*

Raja MAHI-MITRA.

Plate IV., Fig. 8. Æ. 0·8. Weight 34 grains. Author.

Obv.—Elephant with uplifted trunk moving to l. Árian legend, *Rajna Mahi-Mitasa.*

Rev.—Man standing to front, spear in r. hand, snake to r. Arian legend, [*Rajna Ma*]*hi Mitasa.*

Plate IV., Fig. 9. Æ. 0·7. Weight 51 grains. Author.

Obv.—Elephant moving to l. with man on his back. Indian legend, *Râjanya Mahi-Mitasa.*

Rev.—Man standing to front with spear in r. hand. Arian legend [*Ra*]*jna Mahi-Mitasa.*

Plate IV., Fig. 10. Æ. 0·75. E. T.'s Prinsep. [Pl. XLIV. 1.]

Obv.—Male figure to front with spear in r. hand, snake to r.

Rev.—Figure on Elephant to l. Arian legend, *Maharajasa Dhara* (?).

Plate IV., Fig. 11. Æ. 0·75. E. T.'s Prinsep. [Pl. XLIV. 19.]

Obv.—Humped Bull to l., symbol over back.

Rev.—Male figure to front. Arian legend, *Maharajasa Janapa* (*dasa*).

N.B.—A coin of similar types, E. T.'s Prinsep (XLIV. 18), has the same legend in Indian letters.

Raja Bhanu-Mitra.

Plate IV., Fig. 12. Æ. 0·55. Weight 32 grains. Author.

Obv.—Elephant to l. Arian legend, *Rajna Bhânu Mitasa.*

Rev.—Bodhi Tree and two Symbols, snake below. Indian legend, [*Rajna*] *Bhânu Mitasa.*

Plate IV., Fig. 13. Æ. 0·4. Weight 16 grains. Author.

Obv.—Symbols as on reverse of figure 12. Indian legend, *Bhânu Mitasa.*

Rev.—Rayed disc of Sun (*Bhânu*) above a Buddhist railing.

Raja Vira Yasas.

Plate IV., Fig. 14. Æ. 0·75. Weight 57·5 grs. Author.

Obv.—Wheel surrounded by circle of dots. Indian legend, *Râjna Koputasya* (or *Koptanasya*) *Vîra Yaṣasya.*

Rev.—*Chaitya* surmounted by Buddhist symbol of *Dharma-chakra* and *Triratna*, with *Swastika* to l., and unknown Buddhist symbol to r. In field the Arian letters *Râjna.*

Raja Vrishni.

Plate IV., Fig. 15. AR. 0·6. Weight 32 grains. Author.

Obv.—Pillar, with half Lion and half Elephant, surmounted by *Triratna* symbol, and surrounded by Buddhist railing. Indian legend, *Vṛishṇi Raja jnâgaṇasya bhubharasya.*

Rev.—Large *Dharma-chakra* symbol. Arian legend, *Vrishni Raja jnâganasya bhubharasya.*

Kuninda.

Plate V.

The Kuniṇḍas, or Kuliṇḍas, would seem to have occupied the hill districts on both sides of the Satlej from time

PLATE V.

KUNINDA.

KOSAMBI.

immemorial. On the coins they call themselves *Kuṇinda*, and this also is the spelling of Varâha Mihira (*Bṛi. Sanh.* xiv. 32, 33), who locates them with the *Kulûtas* and *Sairindhas*, or the people of Kullu and Sarhind. In another place he locates them to the east of the Madras (*Madreso anyaṣcha Kauṇiṇḍaḥ*). In Ptolemy I find the name of *Kulindrine*, and this spelling is suggested by the *Kuliṇḍâ* of the Vishnu Purâna, and the *Kauliṇḍa* of the Mârkandeya Purâna. From their position I have no hesitation in identifying them with the *Kunets* of the present day, who number not less than 400,000 persons, and form the bulk of the population in Kullu, and all the hill districts around Simla.[45]

As before, the greater number of their coins are found in the country between Ambâla and Sahâranpur. I think it probable that their capital may have been at *Srughna* (or *Sugh*) on the west bank of the old Jumna, where the high road from the Punjâb to the eastward had crossed the river for many centuries.

The earliest coins are distinguished by Buddhist symbols only in addition to the name of Kuṇiṇḍa; but the later coins have the trident and battle-axe of Siva, and want the tribal name.

There is a single coin of very early date, Plate V. fig 6, which is of doubtful attribution, but as it was found in company with the known coins of the Kunindas, I think it best to describe it along with them.

Plate V., Fig. 6. Æ. 0·9. Weight 110 grains. Author.

Obv.—Tall Bodhi tree in Buddhist railing, temple to l., surmounted by *Tri-ratna* symbol. Indian legend to r. in Asoka letters, *Kâdasa*. A subdivision of the Kunets is named *Kaḍaik*, from an ancestor called *Kaḍu* or *Kaḍru*.

---

[45] See *Archæol. Survey of India*, xiv. 126.

Rev.—Large rayed circle of the Sun.

Plate V., Fig. 1. Æ. 0·7. Weight 34 grains. Author.

Obv.—Deer to r., Buddhist symbol between horns, *Chaitya* between legs, symbol over back; to r. female figure holding flowers towards the Deer. Indian legend, *Rajna Kunindasa Amogha-bhûtisa Mahârajasa.*

Rev.—Chaitya surmounted by combined *Tri-ratna* and *Dharmachakra* symbols; snake below; tree and Buddhist railing to r.; Swastika and symbol to l. Arian legend, *Rajna Kunindasa Amogha-bhûtisa Mahârajasa.*

N.B.—The reading of *Kuninda* was made by me in 1868, and published in the Academy in 1874. It was afterwards, in 1875, adopted by Mr. E. Thomas without acknowledgment.

Plate V., Fig. 2. Æ. 0·7. Weight 34 grains. Author.

Types and legends same as No. 1, but there is no Chaitya between the Deer's legs.

Plate V., Fig. 3. Æ. 0·8. Weight 75 grains. Author.

Types same as silver coins Nos. 1 and 2, but Indian legend only on obverse. A few of the larger copper coins have both legends; many of the smaller coins have no legend.

Plate V., Fig. 4. Æ. 0·85. Weight 131 grains. Author.

Obv.—The God Ṣiva, standing to front with battle-axe trident in r. hand, and leopard skin hanging from l. arm. Indian legend, *Bhâgavato Chatreswara Mahâtanâ.*

Rev.—Deer in middle with symbol between horns, snake below to r., tree, star and vase to l. Chaitya and symbols.

Plate V., Fig. 5. Æ. 1·0. Weight 291 grains. Author.

Types and legends same as last.

N.B.—These two coins are extremely rare. Only five specimens are known to me. The reverse of one of them was published by James Prinsep [see E. Thomas, I., Plate XX., fig. 48]. All the five coins came from the west of the Jumna.

Kosambi.

Plate V.

The famous old city of *Kosambi* is now represented by a grand ruined fort on the Jumna with its two villages of *Kosam-Inâm* and *Kosam-Khirâj*, or "Rent-free" and "Rent-paying" Kosam.[46] It is just 31 miles above the fort of Allahabad. It was the capital of the *Vatsas*, and was, therefore, generally known as *Vatsa-pattana*, or the "Vatsa city." On the north-west stands the holy hill of Prabhâsa, with its dragon cave, and inscription of Raja *Baha-sata-mitra*, whose coins will be described presently.

The earliest coins of Kosam are all cast pieces, of which Nos. 7, 8, 9 and 10 of Plate V. are good examples.

Plate V., Fig. 7. Æ. 1·0. Weight 104 grains. Author.

Obv.—Humped Bull moving to l. towards a standing symbol.

Rev.—Bodhi tree with Buddhist railing in middle, wheel to l., Swastika to r., and Chaitya below. A very good specimen of this coin is given by James Prinsep [E. Thomas, II. Pl. XLIV., fig. 6].

Plate V., Fig. 8. Æ. 1·0. Weight 68 grains. The mould was broken across.

Obv.—Horse moving to r. towards a square. Indian legend at top, [*Baha*]*sata Mitasa.*

Rev.—Elephant, with upraised trunk, moving to r., tree and Chaitya behind.

---

[46] *Archæol. Survey of India*, i. 301.

Plate V., Fig. 9. Æ. 1·1. Weight 100 grains. Author.

Obv.—The Goddess Lakshmi standing in a lotus flower to front; on each side, standing on a small lotus flower, an Elephant, with upraised trunk, anointing the goddess.

Rev.—Bodhi tree with Buddhist railing in middle. Unknown symbols on each side.

Plate V., Fig. 10. Æ. 1·0. Weight 190 grains. Author.

Obv.—Elephant standing to l. between two symbol pillars. Indian legend above, *Sudevasa.*

Rev.—Bodhi tree to r. Unknown symbols to l.

Raja BAHASATA MITRA.

Plate V., Fig. 11. Æ. 0·75. Weight 98 grains. Author.

Obv.—Bodhi tree with Buddhist railing in middle, symbols on each side. Indian legend, *Bahasata Mitasa.*

Rev.—Humped Bull moving to r. towards Chaitya raised on Buddhist railing. Ujain symbol above.

Plate V., Fig. 12. Æ. 0·75. Weight 95 grains. Author.

Coin of *Bahasata Mitasa* countermarked with Buddhist Triratna symbol.

Plate V., Fig. 13. Æ. 0·7. Weight 121 grains. Author.

Coin of *Bahasata Mitra* countermarked with symbol standing on Buddhist railing.

Raja ASWA GHOSHA.

Plate V., Fig. 14. Æ. 0·65. Weight 21 grains. Author.

Obv.—Bodhi tree between snake and unknown symbol. Indian legend, *Aswa-ghoshasa.*

Rev.—Symbols uncertain.

Raja JETHA MITRA.

Plate V., Fig. 15. Æ. 0·7. Weight 89 grains. Author.

PLATE VI.

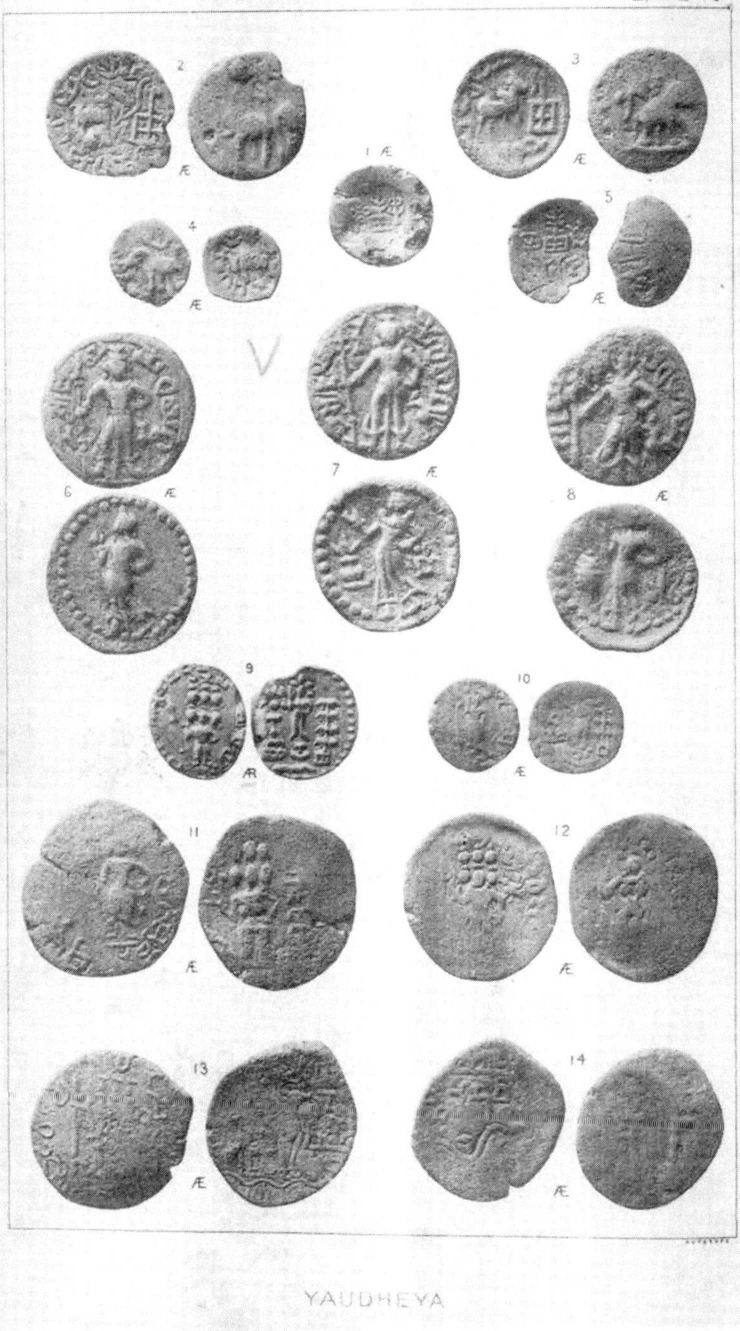

YAUDHEYA

Obv.—Male figure standing to front, r. hand raised, l. hand on hip. Indian legend to r., *Jetha Mitasa.*

Rev.—Indistinct animal, like horse.

Plate V., Fig. 16. Æ. 0·7. Weight 127 grains. Author.

Obv.—Bodhi tree with Buddhist railing in middle, symbols on each side. Indian legend below, *Jetha Mitasa.*

Rev.—Indistinct.

Plate V., Fig. 17. Æ. 0·6. Weight 59 grains. Author.

Obv.—Small Chaitya and Ujain symbol. Indian legend, *Jetha Mitasa.*

Rev.—Indistinct.

Plate V., Fig. 18. Æ. 0·8. Weight 60 grains. Author.

Obv.—Bodhi tree in middle. Indian legend, *Raja Dhana Devasa.*

Rev.—Humped Bull to l., trident and Chaitya.

N.B.—Small coins of this last type with Bull and Bodhi tree are very numerous. The inscriptions are always short, and apparently incomplete. A few specimens were given by James Prinsep [E. Thomas, I. Pl. VIII., fig. 12, 13, 14, 15].

YAUDHEYA.

Plate VI.

The *Yaudheyas* were one of the most famous tribes of Ancient India. They were especially noted as warriors; their name, in fact, meaning simply "soldier or fighter" from *Yudha*, "battle." As they are mentioned by Pânini, before the time of Alexander, as one of the warlike tribes of the Panjâb, we ought to find their name amongst the opponents of the Macedonian leader. They now occupy the country on both banks of the Satlej, and the lower Doab between the Satlej was named after them, the *Johiya-bâr*. This is the present form of the name, as derived from *Jodhiya,* which is the usual pronunciation of *Yaudheya.* Other *Johiyas* are also found in the Salt Range, and I conclude that Mount *Judh,* of the Salt Range, must have received its name from them.

Quintus Curtius mentions a tribe named *Sambracæ,* or *Sabracæ,* who had no king, but were led by "three" generals. Orosius calls them *Sabagræ.* Now the coins of the Yaudheyas show that they were divided into three tribes, and as *Vâgar* means a "warrior," it is possible that the three tribes may have been called *Sam-vâgri,* or the "United Vâgars." The great fort of Bhatner is in *Bâgar-deṣ,* and the Bikaner Raja was called "*Bâgri Rao*" by Akbar. In the same districts also are the *Bhaṭis,* who derive their name from *Bhaṭa,* a "warrior." It seems, therefore, not unnatural to conjecture that the three "warrior tribes" of *Johiyas, Bâgris,* and *Bhaṭis,* map be only divisions of the great clan of Yaudheyas, or *Samvâgris.*

Rudra Dâma, the Satrap of Surashtra, boasts in his Junâgarh inscription of having "rooted out the Yaudheyas," about A.D. 150, but as they are mentioned in the Samudra Gupta inscription on the Allahabad Pillar, they were still powerful about A.D. 470.

The coins of the Yaudheyas are found in the Eastern Punjab, and all over the country between the Satlej and Jumna Rivers. Two large finds have been made at *Sonpath,* between Delhi and Karnâl. The coins are of two distinct kinds; the older ones, of small size, dating from about the first century B.C., and the later ones, of large size, dating from about A.D. 300, after the decline of the Indo-Scythian power. The figures on these later coins are certainly copied from the Indo-Scythian money.

A third class, beginning with the silver coin No. 9, Plate VI., are, perhaps, of a slightly later date. They are remarkable for having a six-headed figure on one side. This figure ought to be Kârtikeya, the son of Siva, who is named *Shadânana* and *Shan-mukhi*, or "six-headed." These later coins must, therefore, be Brahminical.

Plate VI., Fig. 1. Æ. 0·4. Weight 23 grains. Author from Behat.

This is a single-die coin, the reverse being blank. The type is a Bodhi tree with Buddhist railing, and four small circles.

Plate VI., Figs. 2, 3. Æ. 0·7. Weight 57 to 70 grains. Author, Behat.

Obv.—Humped Bull to r. approaching a Bodhi tree with railing. Indian legend in two parts, over and under the bull, the latter imperfect, the former *Yaudheyanâ* (or *ni*).

Rev.—Elephant walking to r. Combine symbol of *Tri-ratna* and *Dharma-chaka.*

Plate VI., Fig. 4. Æ. 0·5. Weight 22 grains. Author.

Same types and legend as Nos. 2 and 3.

Plate VI., Fig. 5. Æ. 0·7. Broken. Author.

Obv.—Bodhi tree between two symbols. Indian legend, *Mahârâja(sa).*

Plate VI., Figs. 6, 7, 8. Æ. 0·9. Mean weight 172 grains. Author.

Obv.—Soldier standing to front, spear in r. hand, l. hand on hip; cock in field to r. Indian legend, *Yaudheya gaṇasya jaya.*

Rev.—Male figure to l., with l. hand on hip and r. hand extended.

Figure 7 has *dwi* after *jaya*, and figure 8 has *tri*.

Figure 7 has two symbols on reverse, one being a vase of flowers.

Figure 8 has also two symbols on reverse, one being a shell.

Plate VI., Fig. 9. AR. 0·7. Weight 26 grains. Author.

Obv.—Six-headed male figure standing to front, with spear in right hand. Indian legend, *Bhâgavato Swâmina Brâhmana Yaudheya.*

Rev.—Six-headed figure standing to front between *Chaitya* and Bodhi tree.

Plate VI., Fig. 10. Æ. 0·6. Weight 30 grains. Author.

Same types as No. 9; inscription incomplete.

Plate VI., Fig. 11. Æ. 1·0. Weight 158 grains. Author.

Obv.—Six-headed figure as on No. 9. Indian legend (completed from many coins), *Bhâgavata Swâmina Brâhmana Devasya.*

Rev.—Six-headed figures, with symbols, as on Nos. 9 and 10.

Plate VI., Fig. 12. Æ. 1·0. Weight 180 grains. Author.

Similar to No. 11, but the *obv.* figure has a small bird on shoulder, and the *rev.* figure appears to be a female.

Plate VI., Fig. 13. Æ. 0·95. Weight 139 grains. Author.

Obv.—As figure 9, and same legend.

Rev.—Antelope to r., with Buddhist symbol over head, and Chaitya to r., and over the back of the deer the letters *darma.*

Plate VI., Fig. 14. Æ. 0·9. Weight 126 grains.

Obv.—A Snake with Indian legend, *Bhânu Varma.*

Rev.—Nearly obliterated; trident visible.

N.B.—The silver coin, fig. 9, determines these coins to

PLATE VII

PANCHÁLA

belong to the *Yaudheyas.* I obtained four of them in the Kangra district; but the silver piece, and upwards of 300 copper pieces, were all found between the Satlej and Jumna Rivers.

PANCHÂLA.

Plate VII.

According to the Mahâbhârata the ancient kingdom of Panchâla extended from the Himâlayan Mountains to the Chambal River. It was divided into North and South Panchâla. The former embraced the whole of Rohilkhand to the north of the Ganges, while the latter included the upper half of the Doab between the Ganges and Jumna. The capital of North Panchâla was *Ahichhatra,* which still exists as a large ruined fortress, twenty miles to the west of Bareli. The capital of South Panchâla was *Kâmpilya,* now Kampil on the Ganges, nearly opposite Badaon.

As the coins which I am now about to describe are found in Rohilkhand, and chiefly at Ahichhatra, Aonla, and Badaon, it is quite certain that they belong to North Panchâla. It has been suggested that they belong to the *Sunga* kings, who ruled over North India after the Mauryas for 112 years, or from B.C. 178 to 66. But the assignment is uncertain, as only one of the coin names, Agni-mitra, is found in the Puranic lists of the Sungas. The dates, however, agree, as all the coins have inscriptions in Asoka characters. I incline rather to assign the coins to a local dynasty of Princes, as they are very rarely found beyond the limits of the North Panchâla, which would not be the case did they belong to the paramount dynasty of the Sungas.

I have found two inscriptions of the Sunga king, *Danabhûti*, at Bharhut and at Mathura, but as his name does not occur in the Puranic lists it is certain that these lists must be incomplete, and perhaps erroneous. As all other Puranic lists have been found to be erroneous, it is possible that these coins from Panchâla may belong to the Sunga kings.

In the Sanskrit drama of *Mâlavikâgnimitra*, translated by Wilson, Agnimitra, son of Pushpamitra, and father of Vasumitra, is called king of *Vidisa* on the *Vetravati*, that is of Besnagar on the Betwa River. As these three names head the lists of the Sunga kings, it would seem that the *Sungas* were rulers of East Mâlwa. As Bharhut, where the Sunga inscriptions of King Danabhûti and his son were found, is much nearer to Besnagar than to Rohilkhand, this assignment is very probable. I conclude, therefore, that the coins found in Rohilkhand are those of some local dynasty and not of the paramount Sunga kings.

All these Panchâla coins are of copper. On one side the die, consisting of the symbols with the name of the king below, is deeply sunk. The letters are somewhat later then Asoka's date, but, I think, earlier than the Christian era. The reverse, which is not sunk, has either a symbol mounted on a Buddhist railing, or the figure of some god, as Agni or Indra, referring to the name of the king.

It is worthy of notice that the weights of the Panchâla coins do not correspond with the common Hindu standard of the *Pana* of 80 ratis or 144 grains and its multiples and divisions, but rather with a centenary piece of 100 ratis, or 180 grains. They agree, therefore, with the heavy standard of the double-die coins of Taxila, which was adopted for the copper coinage of Pantaleon and Agathokles. Instead of inventing new names I prefer to adhere to the old Hindu system, and to call the 100-*rati* or 180-grain coin a heavy *paṇa*, equal to 1¼ *paṇa* of the common standard. The multiples and subdivisions are few in number, and comprise only the following specimens:—

The single heavy *paṇa*	of	100	ratis or	180	grains
1½	,,	150	,,	270	,,
½	,,	50	,,	90	,,
¼	,,	25	,,	45	,,
⅛	,,	12½	,,	22½	,,

RUDRA-GUPTA.

Plate VII., Fig. 1. Æ. 0·75. Weight 78 grains. Author.

Obv.—Incuse square, with three symbols above and Indian legend below, *Rudra Guptasa*. The reading of Rudra is not quite certain. At first I read *Chandra*. The coin is earlier than any of the Mitras.

Rev.—Trident, fixed on basement of Buddhist railing.

Plate VII., Fig. 2. Æ. 0·55. Weight 32 grains. Author.

Types and legend as on figure 1.

N.B.—Rudra is a name of *Ṣiva*, whose symbol is a trident.

DHRUVA-MITRA.

Plate VII., Fig. 3. Æ. 0·7. Weight 53 grains. Author.

Obv.—Incuse square, with the three Panchâla symbols Indian legend below, *Dhuva Mitasa*.

Rev.—Trident on basement of Buddhist railing.

N.B.—*Dhruva* is the North Polar Star, but as it is also a name of Ṣiva, I conclude that the trident refers to him.

SURYA-MITRA.

Plate VII., Fig. 4. Æ. 0·85. Weight 228 grains. Author.

Obv.—Incuse square, with three Panchâla symbols. Indian legend, *Suya-Mitasa.*

Rev.—Rayed circle of "Sun," on altar above Buddhist railing.

PHALGUNI-MITRA.

Plate VII., Fig. 5. Æ. 0·85. Weight 186 grains. Author.

Obv.—Incuse square, with three Panchâla symbols. Indian legend, *Phaguni Mitasa.*

Rev.—Female figure standing to front. Perhaps the constellation, *Phalguni* personified.

BHÂNU-MITRA.

Plate VII., Fig. 6. Æ. 0·35. Weight 182 grains. Author.

Obv.—Incuse square, with three Panchâla symbols. Indian legend, *Bhânu Mitasa.*

Rev.—Rayed circle of the "Sun" (*bhânu*) on Buddhist basement.

— Fig. 7. Coin of Bhânu Mitra, with the central symbol obliterated by countermark of r. hand symbol.

— Fig. 8. Coin of Bhânu Mitra, with all the Panchâla symbols obliterated by countermark of full length figure.

Plate VII., Fig. 9. Æ. 0·5. Weight 18 grains. Author. Also 35 grains.

Types and legend as No. 6.

BHADRA-GHOSHA.

Plate VII., Fig. 10. Æ. 1·0. Weight 252 grains. Author.

Obv.—Incuse square, with three Panchâla symbols. Indian legend, *Bhadra Ghosasa.*

Rev.—Standing figure, almost defaced.

Plate VII., Fig. 11. Æ. 0·4. Weight 16 grains.

Obv.—As No. 10; letters very perfect.

Rev.—Female figure standing to front.

BHÛMI-MITRA.

Plate VII., Fig. 12. Æ. 0·85. Weight 198 grains.

Obv.—Incuse square, with three Panchâla symbols. Indian legend, *Bhûmi Mitasa.*

Rev.—Figure, standing on Buddhist railing; head with five rays.

N.B.—The figure is probably that of *Bhûmi*, or the earth personified.

AGNI-MITRA.

Plate VII., Fig. 13. Æ. 0·9. Weight 291 grains. Author.

— Fig. 14. Æ. 0·45. Weight 34 grains. Author.

— Fig. 15. Æ. 0·65. Weight 89 grains. ,,

Obv.—Incuse square, with three Panchâla symbols. Indian legend, *Agi-Mitasa.*

Rev.—Male figure, with five-rayed head, standing on Buddhist railing.

N.B.—The figure is probably *Agni*, or God of Fire, with five flames.

Plate VII., Fig. 16. Æ. 0·4. Weight 22 grains. Author.

Obv.—Bodhi tree and railing. Indian legend, [*A*]*gi-Mitasa.*

Rev.—Humped Bull, moving to left.

N.B.—This coin may, perhaps, belong to the Panjâb.

JAYA-MITRA.

Plate VII., Fig. 17. Æ. 0·6. Weight 65 grains. Author.

Obv.—Incuse square, with three Panchâla symbols. Indian legend, *Jaya-Mitasa.*

Rev.—Figure, on Buddhist basement

Viswa-Pala.

Plate VII., Fig. 18. Æ. 0·65. Weight 58 grains. Author.

Obv.—Incuse square, with three Panchâla symbols. Indian legend, *Viṣa Pâlasa.*

Rev.—Indistinct.

Indra-Mitra.

Plate VII., Fig. 19. Æ. 0·6. Weight 66 grains. Author.

Obv.—Incuse square, with three Panchâla symbols. Indian legend, *Idra-Mitasa.*

Rev.—Figure of Indra seated on Buddhist railing.

Plate VII., Fig. 20. Æ. 0·5. Weight 54 grains. Author.

Obv.—As No. 19.

Rev.—Figure of Indra inside Temple.

Vishnu-Mitra.

Plate VII., Fig. 21. Æ. 0·55. Weight 60 grains. Author.

Obv.—Incuse square, with three Panchâla symbols. Indian legend, *Vishnu Mitasa.*

Rev.—Four-armed figure (Vishnu) standing on Buddhist basement.

N.B.—From this detailed examination of their coins, I conclude that the Rajas of Panchâla were certainly Brâhminists, as there is an entire absence of Buddhist symbols, coupled with the use of Brahminical names, such as Rudra and Vishnu, Indra, Agni, and Surya. It must be remembered also that *Ahi-chhatra*, the name of the capital of North Panchâla, was the altered form used by the Buddhists instead of the original *Adi-kshetra* of the Brahmins.

PLATE VIII.

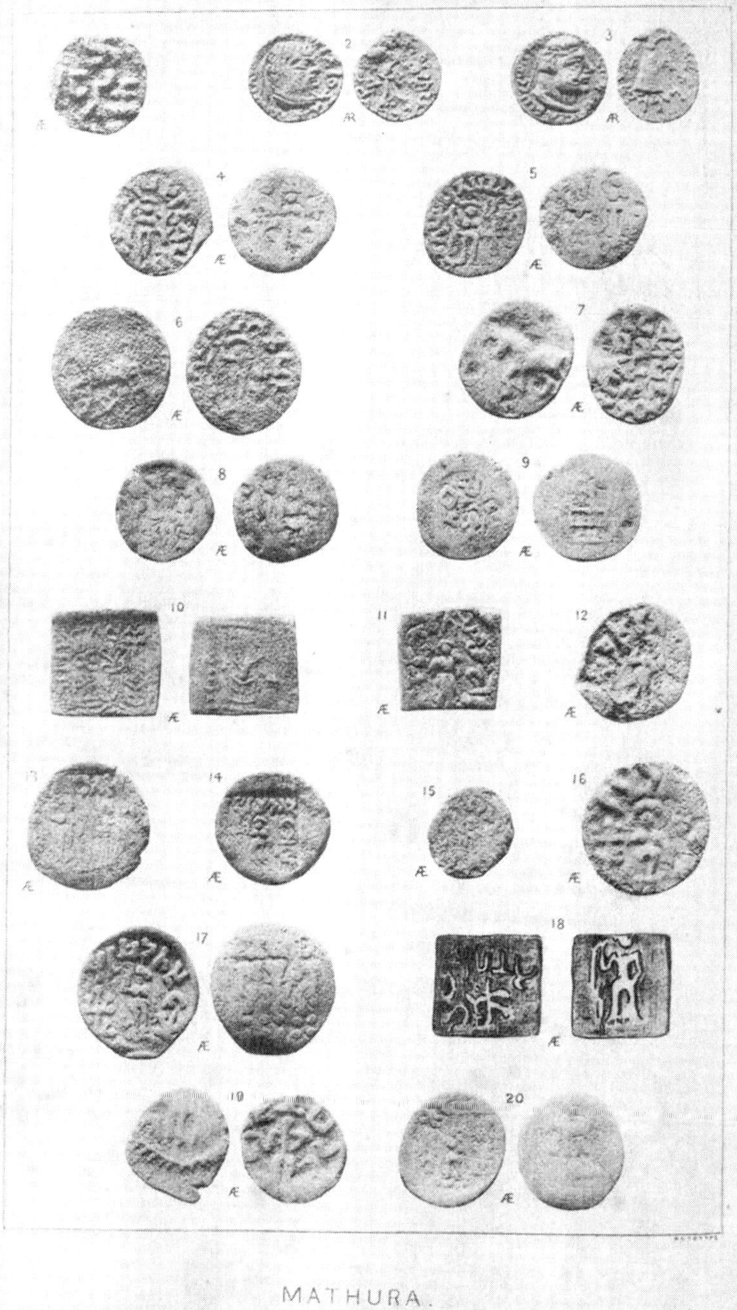

MATHURA.

MATHURA.

Plate VIII.

The holy city of Mathura, which Ptolemy calls Μόδουρα ἡ τῶν Θεῶν, stands on the bank of the Jumna, 35 miles to the North of Agra. Ancient coins are found here in great numbers, beginning with the Greek hemi-drachms of Mennander, Apollodotus, and Antimachus II. The coins of the Kushân Indo-Scythians are still more numerous; and as many of their inscriptions have been dug up in the ruins, there can be no doubt that Mathura belonged to their dominions. In fact, Ptolemy includes Mathura in the kingdom of *Kaspeiria*, which embraced the whole of the lower Punjâb. The Satrapy of Mathura probably extended to Delhi on the North, to Gwalior on the South, and to Ajmer on the West. Many of the coins included in this Plate were brought for sale from the surrounding country. The Chinese Pilgrim, Hwen Thsang, says Mathura was 800 miles in circuit.

The coins given in the accompanying Plate begin with a single specimen, bearing a legend in Asoka characters. Many punch-marked silver coins are also found at Mathura. A few short inscriptions in Asoka letters have been found on Buddhist railing pillars. But the great mass of the antiquities, both of coins and inscriptions, begin with the occupation of the country by the Indo-Scythians.

The coins of the Indo-Scythian Princes are described in another special work dedicated to them alone. In the accompanying Plate I have given coins of four Satraps who flourished during the Indo-Scythian period, namely, *Rajubula* and his son, *Saudâsa*, and *Hagamâsha* and his contemporary (perhaps brother), *Hagâna*. The remaining coins are all of pure Hindu Princes.

Plate VIII., Fig. 1. Æ. 0·65. Weight 30 grains Author.

Obv.—Swastika. Indian legend below, in Asoka letters, *Upatikya.*

Satrap Rajubula.

Plate VIII., Fig. 2. AR. 0·55. Weight 37 grains.

Obv.—Diademed head of king to r. Greek legend, BACIΛЄωC CωTHPOC PAZYBACIΛЄI.

Rev.—Pallas to l., with ægis and thunderbolt. Arian legend, *Apratihatachakrasa chhatrapasa Ranjubulasa.* In field to r. and l. the Arian letters *a* and *g.*

Plate VIII., Fig. 3. AR. 0·55. Weight 36 grains.

Obv.—Diademed head as Fig. 2, but of modern work. Greek legend, BACIΛЄI BACIΛEωC CωTHPOC PAZ.

Rev.—Pallas as on Fig. 2. In field the Arian letters *h* and *sti.* On some specimens a Greek monogram, forming EY, or EYAY, as on some coins of Zoilus. Arian legend, *Chhatrapasa apratichakrasa Ranjubulasa.*

N.B.—These coins, 87 in number, were found in 1852 in one of the ruined mounds at Mathura, in company with 96 base hemi-drachms of Straton. Since then I have obtained a few similar pieces in the Eastern Panjâb, along with a number of small copper pieces of the same types.

Plate VIII., Fig. 4. Æ. 0·7. Weight 92 and 90 grains. From Mathura.

Obv.—Figure standing to front, holding snake (?) in r. hand. Indian legend, *Mahâkhatapasa Râjabulasa.*

Rev.—The goddess *Lakshmi* standing to front, with a small elephant on each side, supported on a lotus flower, anointing the goddess with their upraised trunks.

Satrap Saudasa, or Sodasa.

Plate VIII., Fig. 5. Æ. 0·75 and 0·65. Weights 90 and 47 grains. Mathura.

Obv.—Same figure as on No. 4, with swastika below; double trident in field. Indian legend, *Mahâkhatapasa putasa Khatapasa Saudâsasa.*

Rev.—Goddess and Elephants, as in No. 4.

N.B.—The long Satrap inscription found at Mathura makes Saudâs the son of the Satrap *Rajul* (a contracted form of Rajubul).

SATRAP HAGÂMÂSHA.

Plate VIII., Fig 6. Æ. 0·7. Weights 61 and 55.

Obv.—Naked horse to l.

Rev.—Figure standing to front, with r. hand raised. Indian legend, *Khatapasa Hagâmâshasa.*

SATRAPS HAGÂNA AND HAGÂMÂSHA.

Plate VIII., Fig. 7. Æ. 0·7. Weight 65 grains.

Obv.—Naked horse to l.

Rev.—Standing figure. Indian legend in three lines, *Khatapâna Hagâna Hagâmâshasa.*

N.B.—I take *Khatapâna* to be the Pali form of the genitive plural *Khatapânâm*, "of the Satraps," whose names follow *Hagâna* and *Hagâmâsha*. The latter name reminds me of *Arimazes* and *Sparamizes*, or *Parmizes*, and points to the foreign origin of these two Satraps.

RAJA BALA-BHUTI.

Plate VIII., Fig. 8. Æ. 0·65. Weight 81 grains.

Obv.—Figure standing to front, with r. hand raised to head. Indian legend, *Râjna Bala-Bhutisa.*

Rev.—Indistinct.

Plate VIII., Fig. 9. Æ. 0·65. Weight 33 grains.

Obv.—Same figure as on No. 8. Indian legend, *Râjna Bala-Bhutisa.*

Rev.—Bodhi tree surrounded by Buddhist railing.

N.B.—These coins are extremely scarce. I have seen only three.

Raja Gomitra.

Plate VIII., Fig. 10. Æ. 0·7. Weight 89 grains.

Obv.—In middle unknown symbol. To r. Bodhi tree and railing; to l. Taurine symbol. Indian legend, *Gomitasa Bârânâyâ.*

Rev.—Bodhi tree surrounded by Buddist railing.

Plate VIII., Fig. 11. Æ. 0·7. Weight, 124 grains.

Obv.—Standing figure. Bodhi tree to l. Indian legend above, *Gomitasa.*

Rev.—Obliterated.

Brahma-Mitra.

Plate VIII., Fig. 12. Æ. 0·7. Weight ——.

Obv.—Figure to front, with r. arm raised to head. Indian legend, *Brahma Mitasa.*

Rev.—Obliterated.

Raja Râma-Datta.

Plate VIII., Fig. 13. Æ. 0·7. Weight 123 grains.

Obv.—Figure to front with r. arm raised in incuse square. Bodhi tree with railing to r. Indian legend above, *Râjna Râma-datasa.*

Rev.—Indistinct.

Plate VIII., Fig. 14. Æ. 0·65. Weight 96 grains.

Same type and legend as Fig. 13 in incuse square.

Plate VIII., Fig. 15. Æ. 0·55. Weight 59 grains.

Same type and legend as No. 13 in circle.

Rev.—Obliterated.

N.B.—The reverses of these coins, when in good order, show three elephants, one to front and the others facing to r. and l., each with a man mounted on his neck.

Plate VIII., Fig. 16. Æ. 0·75. Weight 90 grains.

Obv.—Figure to front with r. arm raised. Indian legend, *Râmadatasa.*

Rev.—The three elephants with riders nearly obliterated.

Purusha-Datta.

Plate VIII., Fig. 17. Æ. 0·75. Weight ——.

Same types as Fig. 16. Indian legend, *Purusha-datasa.*

Vira-Sena.

Plate VIII., Fig. 18. Æ. 0·6. Weight ——.

Obv.—Symbols indistinct. Indian legend above, *Vîra-Senasa.*

Rev.—Figure to front with r. arm raised.

Raja-Janapada.

Plate VIII., Fig. 19. Æ. 0·7.

Obv.—Humped bull to l.

Rev.—Figure to front with r. arm raised. Indian legend, *Rajna Janapadasa.*

Ârjunâyana.

Plate VIII., Fig. 20. Æ. 0·65. Weight 81 grains.

Obv.—Figure to front, symbol to l. Bodhi tree to r. Indian legend above, *Arjunâyanâna.*

Rev.—Humped bull to l.

N.B.—I find a duplicate of this rare coin of the *Arjunayanas* in Prinsep's Antiquities, by Thomas, Pl. XLIV. fig. 22. The legend was read as *Rajṇa Raghunâm.* The Ârjunâyanas are mentioned as a tribe in Samudra Gupta's Allahabad Pillar inscription. Their name follows that of the Mâlavas and precedes those of the Yaudheyas, and Mâdras. According to this collocation of the names the Ârjunâyanas may have occupied some part of Rajputâna, to the North of Malwa and to the South of Madradesa, or Mâdra. Perhaps *Ajudhan,* on the bank of the old Satlej River, may still preserve some trace of their name.

AYODHYA.

Plate IX.

Ayodhya, the ancient kingdom of Râma, is now known by the shorter name of Oudh (or Âwadh). The old capital of Ayodhya is still known as Ajudhya, and there all the coins in the accompanying Plate IX. were obtained. A few coins of this class have been published by Mr. Carnac, in the Bengal Asiatic Society's Journal for 1880, Plates XVI. and XVII., but without any notice of their findspots. Amongst them is a new type of Visâkha Deva, which I have given in Plate IX., fig. 7.

In my account of Ayodhya[47] I have identified it with the *Visâkha* of the Chinese pilgrim, Hwen Thsang, and I have suggested that this name was perhaps derived from

---

[47] *Archæol. Survey of India*, i. 318.

PLATE IX.

AYODHYA.

the famous lady *Visâkhâ*, the daughter of the rich merchant *Dhananjaya*, of Sâkata or Ayodhya. On some of the oldest coins of Ajudhya will be found the names of *Dhana-deva* and *Visâkha Datta*, which may very plausibly be connected with those of the rich merchant and his daughter. The coins are certainly not older than the second century B.C., but, as both names were popular, they would probably be repeated in many families of Ayodhya. The coins themselves do not present any traces of Buddhism except the Bodhi tree and the combined symbol of the *Tri-ratna* and *Dharma-chakra*. But neither do they show any special traces of Brahmanism, except in the names of Ṣiva and Vâyu.

Plate IX., Fig. 1. Æ. 0·7. Broken.

Obv.—Buddhist symbol surrounded by rayed circle.

Rev.—Plain.

Plate IX., Fig. 2. Æ. 0·5. Weight 34 grains, *Kâkini*, or ¼ *paṇa*.

Obv.—Swastika.

Rev.—Buddhist symbol of four crescents, with circle in middle.

Plate IX., Fig. 3. Æ. 0·5. Weight 38 grains. *Kâkini*, or ¼ *paṇa*.

Obv.—Swastika and fish.

Rev.—Taurine symbol and axe.

Mula-Deva.

Plate IX., Fig. 4. Æ. 0·85. Weight 56 grains. Half-*pana*.

Obv.—Elephant moving to l. towards Buddhist symbol. Indian legend, *Mûla Devasa.*

Rev.—Wreath in centre, snake below. Buddhist symbol above.

Vâyu Deva.

Plate IX., Fig. 5. Æ. 0·80. Weights 86 and 87 grains.

Obv.—Elephant moving to l. Indian legend, *Vâyu Devasa.*

Rev.—Four triratna symbols on four sides of small circle. Bodhi trees to r. and l. Snake below.

Visâkha Deva.

Plate IX., Fig. 6. Æ. 0·75. Weight 45 grains.

Obv.—The goddess Lakshmi standing to front. A small elephant on each side anointing her. Indian legend, *Visâkha Devasa.*

Rev.—Buddhist symbol in middle. Bodhi tree on each side. Snake below. Swastika above.

Plate IX., Fig. 7. Æ. 0·8. Mr. Carnac, Bengal Asiat. Soc. Journal, xlix., Pl. XVI. 2.

Obv.—Humped bull moving to l. Indian legend, *Visâkha Devasa.*

Rev.—Circle with dots in middle. *Tri-ratna* symbol above; snake below; Buddhist symbol on each side.

Dhana Deva.

Plate IX., Fig. 8. Æ. 0·8. Weight, 38 grains; thin coin.

Obv.—Humped bull moving to r. Indian legend, *Dhana Devasa.*

Rev.—Bodhi tree to r.; figure in middle; Swastika to l.

Plate IX., Fig. 9. Æ. 0·75. 103 grains; thick coin.

Obv.—Humped bull moving to l. Indian legend, *Dhana Devasa.*

Rev.—Bodhi tree to r.; Buddhist pillar to left; snake below.

Siva-Datta.

Plate IX., Fig. 10. Æ. 0·6. Weight 24 grains.

Obv.—Elephant moving to l., towards symbol on pillar. Indian legend, *Ṣiva-datasa.*

Rev.—Tree inside railing.

Plate IX., Fig. 11. Æ. 0·6. Weight 20 grains.

Obv.—Elephant and Indian legend as on last.

Rev.—Cross with four circles.

N.B.—All the above are cast coins. The following are die-struck coins.

Satya-Mitra.

Plate IX., Fig. 12. Æ. 0·8. Weight 123 grains.

Obv.—Humped bull to l., facing upright standard.

Rev.—Cock and fan-palm tree standing on snake.

Plate IX., Fig. 13. Æ. 0·45. Weight 27 grains.

Types and legend as on No. 12.

Surya-Mitra.

Plate IX., Fig. 14. Æ. 0·65. Weight 105 grains.

Obv.—Humped bull to l., facing standard. Indian legend, *Su(r)yya Mitasa.*

Rev.—Cock and fan-palm tree as on No. 12.

Plate IX., Fig. 15. Æ. 0·4. Weight 25 grains.

Types and legend as on No. 14.

SANGHA-MITRA.

Plate IX., Fig. 16. Æ. 0·80. Weight 123 grains.

Obv.—Humped bull to l. Indian legend, *Sangha* (*Mitasa*).

Rev.—Front view of temple or shrine (?).

VIJAYA-MITRA.

Plate IX., Fig. 17. Æ. 0·55. Weight 30 grains.

Obv.—Humped bull to l., before standard. Indian legend, *Vijaya Mitasa.*

Rev.—Cock and fan-palm tree.

Plate IX., Fig. 18. Æ. 0·6. Weights 46 and 40 grains.

Obv.—Combined symbol of *Tri-ratna* and *Dharma Chakra.* Indian legend below, *Vijaya Mitasa.*

Rev.—Humped bull to l., standing on railed base.

Plate IX., Fig. 19. Æ. 0·55. Weight 29 grains.

Obv.—*Tri-ratna* symbol. Indian legend, *Vijaya Mitra.*

Rev.—Indistinct object standing on railed base.

UJAIN.

Plate X.

Ujain, in Sanskrit Ujjayini, is one of the most ancient cities in India. It is situated on the Sipra River, 16 miles to the north of Indore, and 120 miles nearly due west from Bhilsa. Much of its importance was derived from its selection by the Hindu astronomers as their first meridian or starting point for measures of longitude. The well-known cities of Kota, Jaypur, Hisar, and Jâ-

PLATE X.

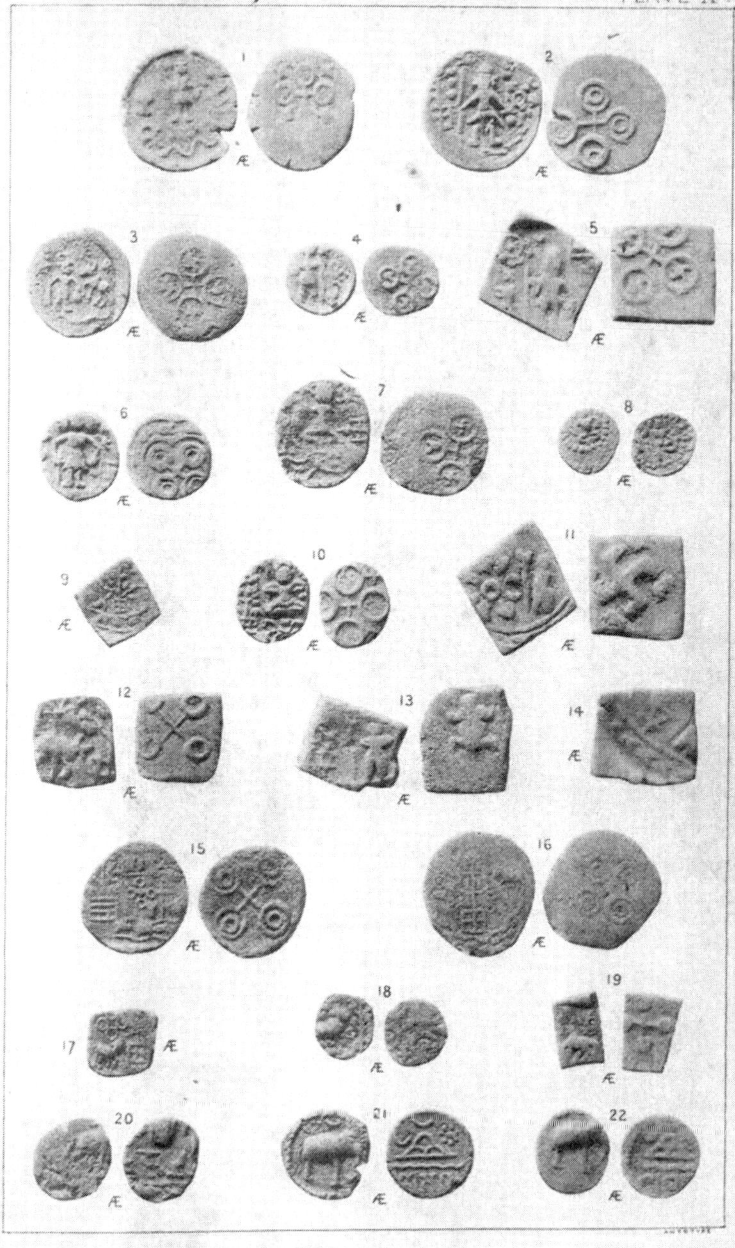

UJAIN.

landhar lie on the same meridian, almost due north of Ujain.

In the beginning of the third century B.C. it was the residence of Asoka, as governor of Mâlwa, under his father, Bindusâra, king of Pâtaliputra. It is renowned as the capital of the great Vikramâditya, who gives name to the era which dates from 57 B.C. About A.D. 80 *Ozene* is described by the author of the Periplus as having formerly been the capital of the country, and in the second century A.D. Ptolemy names it as the capital of *Tiastanes,* who is the great Satrap Chashtan of our coins and inscriptions.

The coins of Ujain are remarkable for a peculiar symbol, which occupies the whole of the reverse. The same symbol, but of small size, is also found on the obverse of a few coins, as on Nos. 15 and 17 of Plate X. This symbol has usually been described as a "cross and balls." It is, in fact, a small cross with a circle at the end of each limb. It occurs also on several of the coins of Eran and Besnagar in East Mâlwa, and may thus point to some political association of the two districts, of which Ujain and Besnagar were the capitals. That they were usually independent states is shown by a most marked difference in their money, the coins of Ujain being invariably round pieces, while those of Besnagar and Eran are nearly all square. Both districts belong to Mâlava at the present day, and we know that the Mâlavas [*Mâlavân* of the early coins] must once have been confederated, as they gave their name to the "era of the Mâlavas," which is now known as the Vikrama Samvat, or "era of Vikramâditya."

As the small coins which bear the name of the *Mâlavâns* are found chiefly in the country 100 miles to the north of Ujain, about Ajmer, Tonk, and Chitor, it seems probable that they may have belonged to same nothern tribe of the Mâlavas. My previous notice of these coins will be found in my *Archæological Survey of India*, Vol. xiv., Plate XXXVI., p. 150. Many of the coins are very small, weighing 8 and 9 grains, and a few only 4 or 5 grains.

The astronomer, Varâha Mihira, places the Mâlavas in the northern division of India, along with the *Madrakas* and *Traigarttas*. This position agrees with the location of the *Mâlwa* Sikhs along the Satlej. Samudra Gupta's inscription on the Allahabad Pillar, A.D. 370, couples the Mâlavas with the Arjunâyanas, Yaudheyas, and Madrakas. The position of the first people is unknown, but the Madrakas, we know, dwelt in the East Panjâb, and the Yaudheyas occupied both banks of the Satlej, the Multân Doâb being still called *Johia-bâr*. These small coins of the Mâlavas have, however, very little in common with those of Ujain and Eran, as they are all inscribed, while the largest do not exceed 25 to 30 grains in weight.

The same "cross and balls" symbol is also found on the coins of some of the Andhra kings of Mahârâshtra, as Vâsithi-putra, Gotami-putra, Yajna Sri, and Vada Sri. In fact Gotami-putra claims Ujain as part of his kingdom, while one of the gateways of the Sânchi Stûpa was erected by Ananda Vâsithi-putra. [See my *Bhilsa Topes*, Plate XIX., fig. 190, and page 264.] The inscriptions on the railing of the Great Stûpa at Sânchi record about twenty gifts from people of Ujain.

I have already noted that the coins of Ujain are nearly all round. In the plate there are several square coins, but I observe that, though the coins themselves are square pieces, yet their impressions were evidently made from *round* dies. The coin, No. 11, is perhaps an interloper from Eran, or East Mâlwa, as similar coins are also found there. The round shape is preserved in the single coin, No. 20, which bears the name of *Ujeniya*, and also in the two dated coins Nos. 21 and 22. I have purchased several specimens of these dated coins at the old town of Sârangpur, 55 miles to the north-east of Ujain, but not a single specimen has yet been found at either Eran or Besnagar.

About the coins themselves very little can be said. In weight they may be arranged in five groups of—

	17	30	53	71	107	grains,
representing coins of	18	36	54	72	108	grains,
which would be	$\frac{1}{8}$	$\frac{1}{4}$	$\frac{3}{8}$	$\frac{1}{2}$	$\frac{3}{4}$	of a *paṇa*.

Not a single specimen of the unit coin, or paṇa, has yet been found at Ujain, although they are not uncommon both at Eran and at Besnagar.

The commonest coins are Nos. 1, 2, 3, 4, 5, on all of which the chief type is a man standing to the front and holding a Sun-standard in his right hand. Beside him there is a tree surrounded by a railing, which shows that these coins were struck during the prevalence of Buddhism. On the opposite side there is an unknown symbol. No. 3 has a humped bull, and on all there is a snake below the standing figure.

On Nos. 7, 8, 10, there is a figure squatted in the native fashion beside a holy tree surrounded by a railing. On the reverse of the small coin, No. 8, there appear three signs or letters, which may read as *mu-bu-mi*.

On No. 9 the holy tree occupies the principal position. Beneath it there are two parallel curved lines, which I guess, but with much hesitation, may, perhaps, represent a river with fish in it. If so, it will be the river *Sipra*, on which Ujain is situated.

No. 6 has a three-headed standing figure, which is probably intended for the Brahmanical god *Mahâkâla*, who had a famous temple at Ujain. The idol worshipped at Ujain as Mahâkâla is mentioned by Al-Beruni,[48] in A.D. 1030. Two centuries later it was carried to Delhi by the Mohammedan conqueror, Iltitmish, and there broken to pieces in front of the great mosque. The figure on the coins seems to carry a club in one hand, and a water vessel in the other, both of which symbols are characteristic of Ṣiva. This coin may, therefore, be accepted as a single evidence of Brahmanism at Ujain.

No. 11 has a large *Swastika,* or mystic cross on one side, with several unknown symbols and the river on the reverse.

No. 12 has a humped bull and tree, with some other symbols.

Nos. 13 and 14 have a large frog on one side, with the Sun-standard, man, and the river, on the reverse.

Nos. 15 and 16 have the holy tree as the chief type, with the river on the first, and a bull on the other.

No. 17 is similar to the last, but square in shape.

No. 18 is small and round, and similar in type to the last.

No. 19 has a horse, with an unknown circular symbol.

No. 20 bears an elephant on one side, and on the reverse a man's hand, with the name of *U-je-ni-ya* below in Asoka characters, not later than 150 B.C.

No. 21 and 22 are dated coins, struck during the sway of the Satraps in Ujain. No. 21 bears the date of 147, and No. 22 has 162, or A.D. 225 and 240. On the obverse is

---

[48] *Sachau's Translation*, i. 202.

ERAKAINA OR ERAN.

an elephant, and on the reverse a *chaitya*, with the sun and moon, as on all the Satrap coins.

ERAN OR ERAKAINA.

Plate XI.

ERAN is an old decayed city on the south bank of the Bîna river, sixteen miles above its junction with the Betwa, fifty miles to the north-east of Bhilsa, and forty-five miles west-north-west from Sâgar. Ancient coins are found here in great numbers. They are all square in form, and offer specimens of the four different classes of old Indian money: (1) Punch-marked coins. (2) Cast coins. (3) Die struck coins. (4) Inscribed coins.

The punch-marked copper coins of Eran are the finest specimens of this class that have yet been found. On all the best coins the punches are confined to one side, and are generally placed quite clear of one another. They are remarkable also for presenting us with the largest and smallest specimens of the old Indian money. One coin, 1·1 inch in breadth, with a corner broken off, weighs 192·5 grains, when perfect it would have weighed about 210 grains, equal to 1½ *paṇa* in value, or 120 ratis of copper. I possess ten coins of the mean weight of 12 grains; ten others of the mean of 8·3 grains; and four coins averaging only 3·25 grains each, being 2 *ratis* of copper, equal to 2 cowrees in value. They are only two-tenths of an inch in diameter.

Similar coins are found in the old ruined capital of Besnagar, situated in the fork between the Betwa and Bes rivers, immediately above their junction, and only a few miles to the west of Bhilsa. It was certainly the capital of east Mâlwa, as Ujain was the capital of west Mâlwa. At Ujain, also, similar coins are found, with a peculiar symbol on the reverse formed of a cross and four balls or circles, the, same as are found on many of the coins in Plate X. Several of the coins are in fact exactly the same; such as Nos. 14 and 17, and others.

The principal types are men, animals, trees, and symbols.

1. MEN; Nos. 16 and 20. On No. 14, the goddess Lakshmi seated, being anointed by two elephants.

2. ANIMALS; the Horse, on No. 1.
Elephant, on Nos. 1, 3, 8, 13.
Bull, on Nos. 11 and 12.
Frog, on coins of Ujain.

3. TREES occur on Nos. 1, 2, 5, 6; on 10, 11, 12, 13, and 19. The trees are probably of different kinds, but as they are nearly all surrounded by a Buddhist railing, they must be intended for Bodhi trees, or the special trees under which each of the Buddhas had sat in meditation before the attainment of Buddhahood.

4. SYMBOLS; these are not easy to describe, but they may be roughly grouped as: (A) Varieties of *Cross and Balls*. (B) Flowers and Ornaments. (C) Buddhist religious symbols. (D) Swastikas. (E) Triangular symbols. (F) Rivers. (G) Cities.

(A.) The cross and balls symbol is found on nearly all the coins of ancient Mâlwa, wherever found—at Eran, Besnagar and Ujain. On some it is small, and the balls or circles are plain. On others the balls are large, and inside each may be either a small swastika, or a taurine symbol, or a small cross and four balls.

(B.) Flower ornaments are of two kinds; the Lotus of eight leaves, on Nos. 2, 6, 10, and the symbol flower of six points, three being arrowheads, and three taurine signs, as on Nos. 4, 16, and 17.

(C.) The Buddhist religious symbols consist of the *Tri-ratna* of three points, and the *Dharma-chakra* wheel, either singly or combined. On No. 17, the combined symbol is quadruple, with the *dharma-chakra* wheel in the middle, and a *tri-ratna* on four different sides.

(D.) The *Swastika* is either plain or ornamental. On No. 15 it is plain, and on No. 20 it is ornamental, with a taurine symbol attached to each arm.

(E.) The triangular symbol consists of a triangle with apex below fixed on the top of a pillar surrounded with a Buddhist railing. It is found in Nos. 2, 3, 4, 5, 8, and 11.

(F.) This peculiar symbol is very common. It consists of two parallel undulating lines forming a narrow channel or passage, in which a continuous stream of small objects, like fish, is shown. It occurs on all the larger coins, with the rare exceptions of a few, like Nos. 9 and 10, which present instead a semi-circle containing fish on No. 10, but only plain round lines on No. 9 and its duplicates. I have conjectured that the long channel may represent the river Bîna on which the town is situated, and that the semi-circle may represent the town itself. The inscribed coin, No. 21, bearing the name of Erakaina or Eran, has the same semi-circular device divided into compartments. Some years ago I suggested that this was intended as a representation of the city itself, as I had found that this same form was used by the tattooers to represent the city of Jhânsi.

Fig. 18 is a thick rude piece of copper weighing 171 grains. It bears the name of *Dhama Pâlasini*, written reversedly in large Asoka characters of early date.

Fig. 21, a small thin copper coin weighing 24 grains.

Obv.—Three concentric circles, the outer two being divided into compartments. Above is a crescent, and, on each side, a tall cross. Over all is the name of the city in early character, *Erakanya,* or simply *Erakana.*

Rev.—Bodhi tree with railing, and the Ujain symbol of cross and balls, with a snake above.

SOUTH INDIA.—ANDHRAS.

Plate XII.

The coins of the Andhras have hitherto been found only to the south of the Narbada River, that is in *Dakshinapatha,* or Dachinabades, or Southern India. But as the later Andhra Kings, according to their own accounts, extended their sway far to the north of the Narbada River, they may be reckoned among the dynasties of North India. The northern countries over which they claim to have ruled are *Surâshtra,* or Kâthiâwâr, *Aparântika,* or West Rajputâna, and *Akarâ-Avanti,* or Ujain of Malwa.

The situation of Aparântika has not yet been settled. Pandit Bhagwân Lâl wished to identify it with the Konkan or Western coast of the Peninsula, and he quotes several authorities to show that it was certainly so esteemed by several writers. One of them, indeed, says that Sopâra was the capital of Aparântika. And so, no doubt, it may have been, just as Bombay is now the capital of Western India. In fact Bombay actually does include Kâthiâwâr and the whole of Sindh, as well as West Rajputâna, which are all to the North of the Narbada.

Aparântika is placed by Varâha Mihira [49] in the *Western*

---

[49] Brihat Sanhita.

PLATE XII.

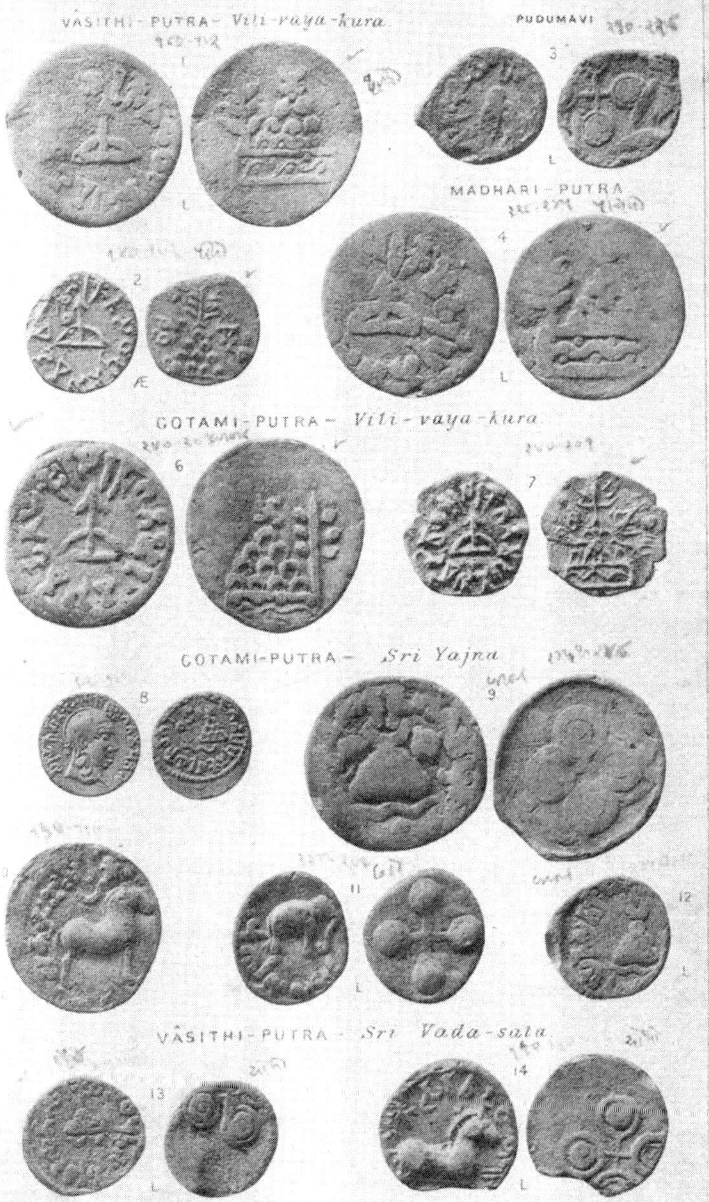

S. INDIA – ANDHRAS

Division of India along with Sindhu-Sauvira and Panchanada, or Sindh and the Panjâb. In the same division he locates Mount *Astagiri*, or the "Western Mountain," which I would identify with Mount Abu. The name of *Aparântika* is perhaps preserved in the *Aratrii* of the Periplus, who held the inland country from Barygaza towards the Arakhosii. This description tallies exactly with the position of West Rajputana, or the provinces of Mewâr and Mârwâr, including Mount Abu. *Aratrii* is an abbreviated form of the Sanskrit *Arâshtra*; but the more usual abbreviation is *Aratta*. By the simple elision of the letter p, which is a common practice in Indian words, the same form is derived from *Aparânta*. Pandit Bhagwân Lâl thought that the first Greek form might have been *Aparatike*, from which was deduced *Ariake*. But the province of Ariake was to the south of the Narbada, therefore corresponds with the Konkan, which is placed by Varâha Mihira in the south-western division of India.

I may add also that the coins of the Aparântikas, bearing the inscription *Apalâtasa Maharâjasa*, were found chiefly in Rajputâna, about Nimach and Ajmer, by Colonel Stacy, while my own specimens have been obtained in North Rajputana and Mathura. For these reasons I conclude that the country known as *Aparântika* or "West Land," was actually in the west of India, and that it did not extend geographically to the south of the Narbada. Politically Sopâra and other places to the south of that river may have been included, just as Delhi and Sahâranpur are now included in the Panjâb, because they have been placed under the Lieutenant Governor of the Panjâb.

Specimens of the coins of Apalâta, or Aparânta, may be seen in Thomas's edition of Prinsep, Pl. XLIV., figs. 25

and 26; and also in Archæol. Survey of India, Vol. XIV., Pl. XXXI., fig. 4.

The earliest notice of Aparântika is in the Pali annals of Ceylon, in the description of the Third Buddhist Synod held during the reign of Asoka in B.C. 241,[50] when missionaries were despatched to all quarters to propagate the Buddhist religion. Amongst them was the Yavana Dharma-Rakshita, who went to *Aparântika*, where he converted 70,000 persons.

I think it probable that the *Oratæ* of Pliny,[51] whose king possessed only ten elephants, but had a large army of foot, may be *Aparâṭas*, as the first part of the name, *or*, is a common abbreviation of *Apar*.

We now come to the inscriptions of the Andhra King, Gotamiputa, and the Ṣaka King, Rudra Dâma.

In line 2 of No. 1 of the Nâsik cave inscription the dominions of Gotamiputa are said to have included the provinces of *Saurâshtra*, *Aparâta* and *Anupa*, or Kathiâwâr West Rajputâna, and Ninâr on the Narbada. In line 6 it is boasted that he had conquered the *Sakas*, *Yavanas* and *Palhavas*, and that he had exterminated the race of *Khagarâta*. In other inscriptions at Nâsik the name of this tribe, written in a Sanskrit form, is *Kshaharâta*. They were under the rule of the Satrap *Nahapâna*, whose date in one inscription is either 46 or 76. As his dominions embraced Prabhâsa, in Kâthiâwâr, as well as Barygâza, to the north of the Narbada, with Sopâra and Nâsik, to the south, his capital was probably at Ujain. In fact, the Jain Chronicles give 17 years to a Saka rule at Ujain from B.C. 57 to 74 when Sâtigâni was Raja of Paithan.[52] If his date be

[50] Mahawanso, p. 71.
[51] *Nat. Hist.*, vi. 23.
[52] Kálakácharya Katha, in *Bombay Journal*, ix. 139.

reckoned from the time of the Saka King, Moas, he must have lived in the middle of the 1st century B.C. That the Kshaharâtas were Sakas is certain, as Ushavadâta, the son-in-law of Nahapâna, calls himself a Saka. I would, therefore, identify the Kshaharâtas with the Sakas, who occupied Ujain in the 1st century B.C.

The descendants of Nahapâna were exterminated by Gotamiputra, the Andhra King, whose capital was at Baithâna (Paithan or Pratisthâna), on the Godâvari. I would identify him with Gotamiputra I., who lived in the 1st century A.D.

The earliest Andhra King of whom we have any coins is *Vâsithi-putra Vilivaya-kura.* He was followed by *Mâdharîputra*, as we learn from the fact of some of his money being struck on pieces of Vâsithi-putra; and, lastly, we learn from a similar cause that *Gotami-putra Sri Yajna* succeeded Mâdhari-putra. The positions and dates of these kings have been discussed by Dr. Bühler in the Indian Antiquary, vol. XII., 273, whose results I have adopted. Pandit Bhagwân Lâl had previously pointed out that Gotamiputra Yajna was the son of a prince named *Vâsithiputra Chatrapana*, whose inscription he had formerly translated.[53]

The inscriptions of Yajna Sri are common, and his reign, according to the Puranic lists, was a long one of 29 years. Dr. Bhau Dâji had previously identified the Saka chief, *Chashtana*, with Ptolemy's *Tiastanes* of Ozene or Ujain. I accept the identification, but not the date which Bhau Dâji assigned to him as a contemporary of the geographer. If any one were to speak of Agra as the "city of Akbar" I should not consider that he intended to make himself a

---

[53] *Bombay Journal*, xii. 407, and xiii. 303.

contemporary of that famous emperor. Similarly, I consider that Ptolemy, who composed his geography from many authorities of several different ages, simply copied the descriptions of his predecessors, without any corrections for difference of age.

On examining all the dates of the coins and inscriptions, I find that the only possible arrangement is to refer them to the Saka era. This conclusion has now been satisfactorily confirmed by the establishment of the Gupta era in A.D. 319. As the Guptas were the undoubted successors of the Western Satraps, the discovery, in a Stûpa deposit, of a coin of the latest Satrap, Swâmi Rudra Sena, son of Satya Sena, whose dates come as low as S. 304, or A.D. 382, in company with a coin of Chandra Gupta Vikramâditya, whose earliest inscription is dated in S. 82 or 318 + 82 = 400 A.D., is clear evidence of their having been contemporaries.

To apply the chronology of the Satraps to the times of the Andhra kings, I would refer to the Junagarh inscription of the Satrap, Rudra Dâma, who boasts of having often defeated the Sâtakarnis. At the same time he claims to have conquered *Akarâvanti* (or east and west Mâlwa), *Anarta* and *Surashtra* (Kathiâwâr), *Sindu Sauvirya* (Sindh), *Aparanta* (west Rajputâna), and *Anupa* (Nimâr), on the Narbada. Now, all these districts had belonged to Gotamiputra I. Sâtakarni, whose reign of twenty-one years I would assign to the first century A.D.

As Rudra-Dâma's inscription is dated in S. 72 or A.D. 150, his warfare with the Sâtakarnis must have taken place about A.D. 130 to 140, or with the predecessors of Yajna Sri.

The following list gives the names of the Sâtakarni kings, from the accession of Gotami-putra I. to the close of the dynasty, with their approximate dates, according to the lengths of reigns given in the Purânas. For comparison, I have given the names of the contemporary Satraps of Surâshtra, with their dates, from coins and inscriptions.

ANDHRAS.			SATRAPS.	
A.D.			A.D.	
78	Gotamiputra I.	Sâtakarni.	78	Chashtana.
99	Pudumayi	Vâsithiputra.	100	Jayadâman.
127	Medhasiras	Madhariputra.	125	Rudra Dâman s. 72 = A.D. 150.
134	Skanda-swâti	Chatrapana.	150	Jiva-Dâman s. 100 = A.D. 178.
141	Yâdna Sri	Gotamiputra II.	178	Rudra Sinha s. 103 = A.D. 118.
170	Vijaya		200	Rudra Sena s. 125 = A.D. 142.
176	Vada Sri	Sâtakarni.	225	Dâma-Sena s. 148 = A.D. 157.
186	Pulomavi.			

The names of *Gotamiputra*, *Vâsithi-putra*, and *Mâdhari-putra* have been explained by Dr. Bühler as matronymics derived from the *Vaidika Gotras* of the Purohitas of the fathers of the queen mothers.[54] Thus, Gotamiputra's mother, Gotamî, derived her name from the Gautama Gotra of her father's Purohita, or family priest. So, also, Vâsithi-putra's mother, Vasithî, got her name from the Vasishtha Gotra of her father's family priest. But no explanation has yet been offered for the curious titles of *Vidivaya-kura* and *Sivâla-kura*, taken by these princes. Perhaps *Sivâla-kura* may have some connection with *Siva-Sri*, the name or title of *Medhasiras* or Madhari-putra.

The types of the coins are few and simple. On all of the early coins, except No. 3, a bow and arrow is the

[54] *Indian Antiquary*, xii. 272.

marked type. These coins were found at Kolhapur in the west.[55] But on most of the others, all of which came from Amaravati, on the Krishna River, the common type is a cross with four balls or circles, which is the well-known symbol on the coins of Ujain. Fig. 7, a silver coin, was found in the Stûpa of Sopâra. Both in weight and in style it corresponds with the coins of the early Satraps, Chashtana, and his successors. A few specimens of the Amaravati, or Eastern coins, have a horse on the obverse, and one specimen has an elephant. But the greater number of the coins present a Stûpa on the obverse. There are a few coins with a lion on one side, and others with a two-masted ship. But on none of them is there any legible inscription.

So far as my experience goes, all the southern coins of the Andhras are found in Eastern India, round about Amaravati, while all the bow and arrow coins come from Western India. My own western specimens I owe to the kindness of my late friends, Pandit Bhagwân Lâl and Mr. Gibbs. My eastern coins I owe to the liberality of Mr. Sewell, who has done so much for the exploration of the antiquities of the Madras Presidency.

Sir W. Elliot was under the impression that the Andhras possessed the whole of the lower valley of the Ganges "from the frontier of Magadha to the sea,"[56] and he quotes Pliny in support of his belief. But the position assigned to them by Pliny is "beyond the Ganges." The whole of the Gangetic valley was then held by the *Prasii* the "most powerful nation in India," who had an army of 600,000 foot and 30,000 horse. As the Andaræ had only 100,000 foot and 3,000 horse, it is quite impossible that

---

[55] The reverse type of the Chaitya and tree occurs on the much earlier coins of Agathokles, of Kabul.

[56] *Coins of South India*, p. 10.

they could have possessed any territory on the Ganges. In Edict XIII. of the Rock inscriptions of Asoka, the Andhras are coupled with the Pulindas, "*Andhra-Pulindeshu.*"

Vâsithi-Putra.

Plate XII., Fig. 1. Lead. 1·2 inch. A.C.

Obv.—Bow, with arrow fixed. Indian legend, *Râjna* Vasithi-putasa *Vidivaya-kurasa.*

Rev.—Large Temple or Chaitya, with tree to l.

Plate XII., Fig. 2. Copper. 0·7 inch. A.C.

Same types and legend as on Fig. 1; in field to l. the combined *Tri-ratna* and dharma-chakra symbols.

Plate XII., Fig. 3. Lead. 0·85 inch. General Pearse.

Obv.—Temple or Chaitya. Indian legend incomplete, *Râjna* [*Vasithiputasa Siri*] *Pudumavasa.*

Madhari-Putra.

Plate XII., Fig. 4. Lead. 1·2 inch.

Obv.—Bow, with arrow fixed, as on No. 1. Indian legend, *Râjna* Madhari-putasa *Sivâla-kurasa.*

Rev.—Temple or Stûpa, raised on plinth, with trees to l.

Plate XII., Fig. 5. Copper. 0·7 inch. A.C.

Same types and legend as on fig. 4.

Gotami-Putra II.

Plate XII., Fig. 6. Lead. 1·15 inch. A.C.

Obv.—Bow, with arrow fixed. Indian legend, *Râjna* Gotami-putasa *Vidivaya-kurasa.*

Rev.—Temple or Chaitya, on plinth, with trees to r.

Plate XII., Fig. 7. Copper. 0·7 inch. A.C.

Same types and legend as on Fig. 6.

Plate XII., Fig. 8. Silver. 0·6 inch, from Stûpa of Sopâra.

Obv.—Head of King to r., with large earrings. Indian legend, *Siri* YAJNA-SATAKANISA *Chatrapana Gotamiputasa.*

Rev.—Stûpa or Temple, with Ujain symbol to l. and sun and moon over symbol; snake below. Indian legend, *Râjna Gotamiputasa Siri* YAJNA-SATAKANISA.

Plate XII., Fig. 9. Lead. 1·1 inch. Weight 240 grains.

Obv.—Chaitya, with shell and flower; snake below. Indian legend, *Râjna Gotamiputasa Siri* YAJNA-SATAKANISA.

Rev.—Ujain symbol of cross and four circles.

Plate XII., Fig. 10. Lead. 0·85 inch. General Pearse.

Obv.—Horse to r., and Indian legend as on No. 9 but incomplete.

Rev.—Ujain symbol.

Plate XII., Fig. 11. Lead. 0·8 inch. Sir W. Elliot.

Obv.—Elephant, moving to r. Indian legend incomplete [*Râjna Gotamiputasa*] *Siri* YAJNA-SA[*takanisa*].

Rev.—Ujain symbol [Coins of S. India. Pl. II., Fig. 43].

Plate XII., Fig. 12. Lead. 0·8 inch. A.C.

Obv.—Temple or Chaitya and snake. Indian legend incomplete, [*Râjna Gotamiputasa Si*]*ri* YAJNA-SATAKANISA.

Rev.—Ujain symbol.

VASITHI-PUTRA—VADA-SATA.

Plate XII., Fig. 13. Lead. 0·7 inch. A.C.

Obv.—Chaitya, with snake. Indian legend, *Râjna Vasithiputasa Siri* VADA-SATASA.

Rev.—Ujain symbol.

Plate XII., Fig. 14. Lead. 0·85. A.C.

Obv.—Horse, to r. Indian legend incomplete, *Râjna Siri* VADA-SA[*tasa*].

Rev.—Ujain symbol.

KÂRWÂR.

A few coins only of Kârwâr have been found by General Pearse. They are of lead and of large size, like the large leaden coins of the Andhras. Only two names are found on the five known specimens. One of each kind has been published in Sir W. Elliot's *Coins of South India.* I have not thought it necessary to give any sketches of them here. But as I read the names differently, I will now describe them.

MUDRA-NANDA, OR MULA-NANDA.

No. 1. Lead. 1·0 inch. Weight 250 grains. Coins of S. India. [Pl. II. 41.]

Obv.—Hemispherical Stûpa, standing on basement, with two rows of niches for lights. Legend in Andhra letters, *Râjna* MUDRA-NANDASA.

Sir W. E. reads, *Madenna Dâsa.*

Rev.—Bodhi tree, surrounded by Buddhist railing; two Buddhist symbols to r., and joint *Tri-ratna* and *Dharma-chakra* to l.

No. 2. *Vadala-Nanda.*

No. 2. Lead. 1·0 inch. Weight 238 grains. Coins of S. India. [Pl. II. 42.]

Obv.—Stûpa, as on No. 1. Legend in Andhra letters, *Râjna* VADALA-NANDASA.

Sir W. E. reads *Vadaka denna Dâsa*, but his letter *K* I take to be the pinnacle of the Stûpa.

Rev.—Tree, as No. 1, with the *Swastika*, and *Tri-ratna* symbols.

NEPAL.

Plate XIII.

NEPÂL is an extensive hilly country, about 500 miles in length by 150 miles in breadth, on the southern slope of the Himâlaya Mountains, between Almora and Darjiling. It embraces all the headwaters of three great rivers, the Sarju, the Gandak, and the Kosi, and is the only part of North India which escaped the tyrannical rule of the Mohammedans. Its ancient capital was Mânagriha, the site of which is unknown; but as all the inscriptions of the Suryavansi dynasty come from the immediate neighbourhood of Deva-pâtana and Kâthmându it was probably only another name for *Deva-pâta* itself, which contained the famous old temple of Paṣupati. *Deva-pâtana* I take to mean only "the god's city," *i.e.*, the city of Paṣupati, or Siva, whose shrine was already in existence when the Suryavansi family of the Lichhavis founded their sovereignty, about the beginning of the Christian era. The genealogical lists have been very fully examined and compared with the inscriptions by Dr. G. Bühler, whose results I accept with perfect confidence. The inscriptions were first discovered and translated by Pandit Bhagwan Lal[57] and Mr. C. Bendall.[58] The dynasty of the Suryan Licchavis ended with Siva Deva after A.D. 634, whose minister, Thâkur Anṣu Varma, a contemporary of the Chinese pilgrim, Hwen Thsang, established the Thakuri dynasty about A.D. 640.

---

[57] *Indian Antiquary.*
[58] *Journey in Nepal and West India.*

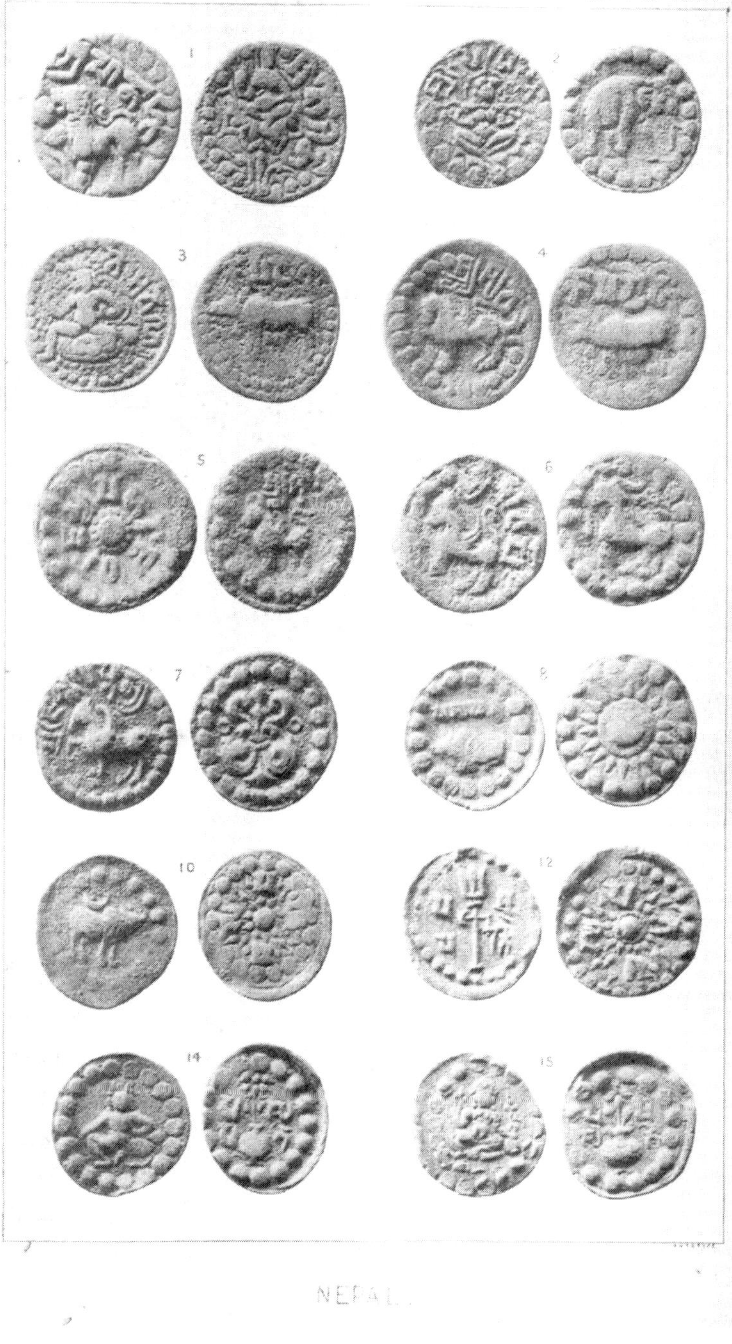

NEPAL.

RAJAS OF NEPÂL.

No.		Samvat.	A.D.	Native List.
1	Jaya Deva	—	1	Kuvera Deva Varma, ninth before Vrisha, 100 A.D.
2 to 12	Eleven names omitted in inscription	—	—	
13	Vrisha Deva	—	260 ?	Vrisha Deva Varma
14	Sankara Deva	—	285 ?	
15	Dharma Deva	—	305	
16	Mána Deva	386—413	329—356	
17	Mahi Deva	—	360 ?	
18	Vasanti Deva	435	378	
19	Udaya Deva	—	400 ?	Udaya Deva Varma
20	Mána Deva V.	—	425	These seven names are supplied from the native lists.
21	Gunakàma Deva V.	—	50	
22	Siva Deva V.	—	75	
23	Narendra Deva V.	—	500	
24	Bhumi Deva V.	—	525	
25	Vishnu Deva V.	—	50	
26	Viswa Deva V.	—	75	
27	———	—	600	
28	Siva Deva II.	—	610 ?	
	THAKURI DYNASTY.			
29	ANṢU-VARMA	Gupt. Sam. 316 Harsha 34-39 45 ?	634 640-645, 651	See Bendall, No. I. Inscr.
30	Dharma Deva (Sri Hasha)	—	—	
31	Jishnu Gupta	46	652	
32	Vishnu Gupta	—	670 ?	
33	Narendra Deva	—	690 ?	
34	Siva Deva II.	119—145	725—751	
35	Jaya Deva II.	153	759	

All the coins that have yet been found are of copper, and of large size. The types seem to be indigenous, and quite different from the contemporary coinage of the Guptas. Perhaps the recumbent bull of the coin of Paṣupati may have been copied from the money of the Guptas and the Nine Nagas. In weight the coins range from 120 grains to 250, corresponding in this respect, as well as in size and style of letters, with the contemporary copper coinage of the Yaudheyas. [See Plate VI.] Both were direct descendants of the copper money of the Kushâns.

The types are few in number. The principal type shows the king seated on a throne holding a flower in his right hand. The positions are varied. Other types are an elephant, a bull either standing or recumbent, a lion sometimes winged, and various circular shields or ornamented solar emblems. Many of the coins of Paṣupati show a vase of flowers, while a few have the trident of Ṣiva with the axe attached to the side. The coins are rather neatly made, the types being generally complete on both sides.

Two copper coins of *Mânangka* were obtained by James Princep in 1833 (*Bengal Journal*, August, 1833, and Thomas Prinsep I., Plate III., fig. 12, and p. 62). No attempt was then made to read them. A coin of Gunângka was published by myself in 1865 (*Journal, Bengal As. Soc.*), and referred to as connected with the various mintages of Pasupati, of whom I made known four specimens.

For most of the early coins in Plate XIII. I am indebted to the kindness of Colonel Warren, who obtained them in Kashmir. According to his list he obtained about a hundred legible coins, and thirty-seven that were unnamed. I was already possessed of twenty-three Nepal coins, of which three were procured at Benares, but the remaining twenty coins were obtained at Gayâ, by purchase in the Bazar, or at Buddha Gayâ in the small votive Stûpas. The Gayâ coins were no doubt obtained by work-people at Buddha Gayâ, and I would therefore ascribe my twenty specimens to the gifts of pilgrims from Nepâl, who visited the holy Bodhi tree during the first six centuries of the Christian era.

The coins of Paṣupati are by far the most numerous, as they form about half of the known specimens of the early Nepalese coinage. The coins of Ansu Varma form about one-fourth, and the remainder are nearly equally divided between Manangka, Gunangka, and Jishnu Gupta. The coins of Paṣupati I was at first inclined to assign to Pasupreksha Deva, who is recorded to have restored the temple of Paṣupati. But as he preceded the establishment of the Suryavansi dynasty, just before the beginning of the Christian era, he would have to be placed several centuries before Mâna Deva. This date is much too early, judging from the style of the letters on the coins, which is unmistakeably Gupta.

Four of the coin names we found on the lists, namely: Manangka, Gunangka, Ansu Varma, and Jishnu Gupta, but there is no trace of Vaisravana. As the name is a patronymic of Kuvera it is possible that he may be the Kuvera Varma of the lists. But, as he is placed nine reigns or generations before Mana Deva, the date of about 100 A.D. seems too early for the style of the coins of Vaisravana (Plate XIII., fig. 4).

Mânângka or Mâna-Deva.

Plate XIII., Fig. 1. Æ. 1·0 inch. Weight, 197 grains. Author.

Obv.—Deity seated on lotus throne; left hand resting on hip; right hand raised upward with expanded fingers. Indian legend in Gupta characters, *Sri Bhogini.*

Rev.—Lion walking to left towards lotus plant, with flower and bird. Indian legend in Gupta letters, *Sri Mânângka.*

Guṇângka or Guṇa-Deva.

Plate XIII., Fig. 2. Æ. 0·9 inch. Weight, 195 and 146 grains. Col. Warren.

Obv.—Goddess seated; right hand held up. Indian legend in Gupta letters, *Sri Guṇângka.*

Rev.—Elephant standing to right.

Vaisṛavaṇa.

Plate XIII., Fig. 3. Æ. 0·95 inch. Weight, 172 grains. Col. Warren.

Obv.—Deity, or Raja, seated to front, holding flower in right hand. Indian legend in Gupta letters, *Vaiṣravaṇah.*

Rev.—Cow to left with calf beneath. Indian legend in Gupta letters, *Kâma-dehi.* This is the cow, usually called *Kâma-dhenu,* which sprang from the churning of the ocean. She possessed the power of granting desires.

Ansụ-Varma.

Plate XIII., Fig. 4. Æ. 0·95 inch. Weight, 212 grains. Col. Warren.

Obv.—Winged lion to l. with left fore-foot raised. Indian legend in Gupta letters, *Ṣryanṣu Varma.*

Rev.—The cow, Kâma-dhenu to l., as on No. 3. Indian legend in Gupta letters, *Kâma-dehi.*

Plate XIII., Fig. 5. Æ. 1·0 inch. Weight, 250 grains. Col. Warren.

Obv.—Round figure of sun with rays. Indian legend in Gupta letters in circle, *Mahârâjâdhirâjasya.*

Rev.—Lion to l., with forefoot raised. Indian legend in Gupta letters, *Sryanṣoḥ.*

Plate XIII., Fig. 6. Æ. 0·95 inch. Weight, 169 grains. Col. Warren.

Obv.—Winged lion to l. with forefoot raised, as on No. 4. Indian legend in Gupta letters, *Sryanṣu Varma.*

Rev.—Lion to l. with forefoot raised. Crescent over back.

Jishnu-Gupta.

Plate XIII., Fig. 7. Æ. 0·9 inch. Weight, 191 grains. Col. Warren.

Obv.—Winged lion to l. with forefoot raised, as on Nos. 4 and 6. Indian legend in Gupta letters, *Sri Jishnu Guptasya.*

Rev.—Ornamental symbol.

Pasupati.

Plate XIII., Fig. 8. Æ. 0·9 inch. Weight, 150 grains. Col. Warren.

Obv.—Recumbent humped Bull to l. Indian legend in Gupta letters, *Paṣupati.*

Rev.—Round sun in middle with large rays.

No. 9. Æ. 0·9 inch. Weight, 114 grains. Col. Warren.

Obv.—Recumbent bull to l. as on Fig. 9, and same legend.

Rev.—Ornamental symbol, as on Fig. 7.

Plate XIII., Fig. 10. Æ. 0·85 inch. Weight, 128 grains. Col. Warren.

Obv.—Humped bull standing to r. Crescent over back.

Rev.—Sun with rays in middle. Indian legend disposed at top and bottom, and r. and l., *Paṣupati.*

No. 11. Æ. Similar types with bull to l. Same legend.

Plate XIII., Fig. 12. Æ. 0·85 inch. Weight, 152 grains. Col. Warren.

Obv.—Trident upright, with axe fixed to l. Indian legend in Gupta letters, in two lines, *Paṣupati.*

Rev.—Sun with rays, and legend disposed as on No. 10.

N.B.—I possess several specimens of lighter weights.

No. 13. Æ. 0·8 inch. Weight, 123 grains. Col. Warren.

Obv.—Trident and legend as on Fig. 12.

Rev.—Sun with rays in middle, surrounded with ornament. No legend.

Plate XIII., Fig. 14. Æ. 0·85 inch. Weight, 95 grains. Col. Warren.

Obv.—King seated with right hand resting on knee.

Rev.—Vase of flowers. Indian legend in two lines, *Paṣupati.*

Plate XIII., Fig. 15. Æ. 0·9 inch. Weight, 114 grains. Col. Warren.

Obv.—King seated with flower in right hand, and holding a vase of flowers in left hand.

Rev.—Vase of flowers and Indian legend, *Paṣupati.*

N.B.—I possess several varieties of these last coins of *Paṣupati;* but the differences are slight, being chiefly confined to the attitude of the Raja, and to the shape and size of the vase. On some the Raja is seated under a canopy.

N.B.—A brief notice of some of these Nepâl coins by Mr. V. Smith and Dr. Hoërnle will be found in the *Proceedings* of the Asiatic Society of Bengal for May, 1887. The coins, about 40 in number, belonged to Dr. Gimlette.

PLATE XIV.

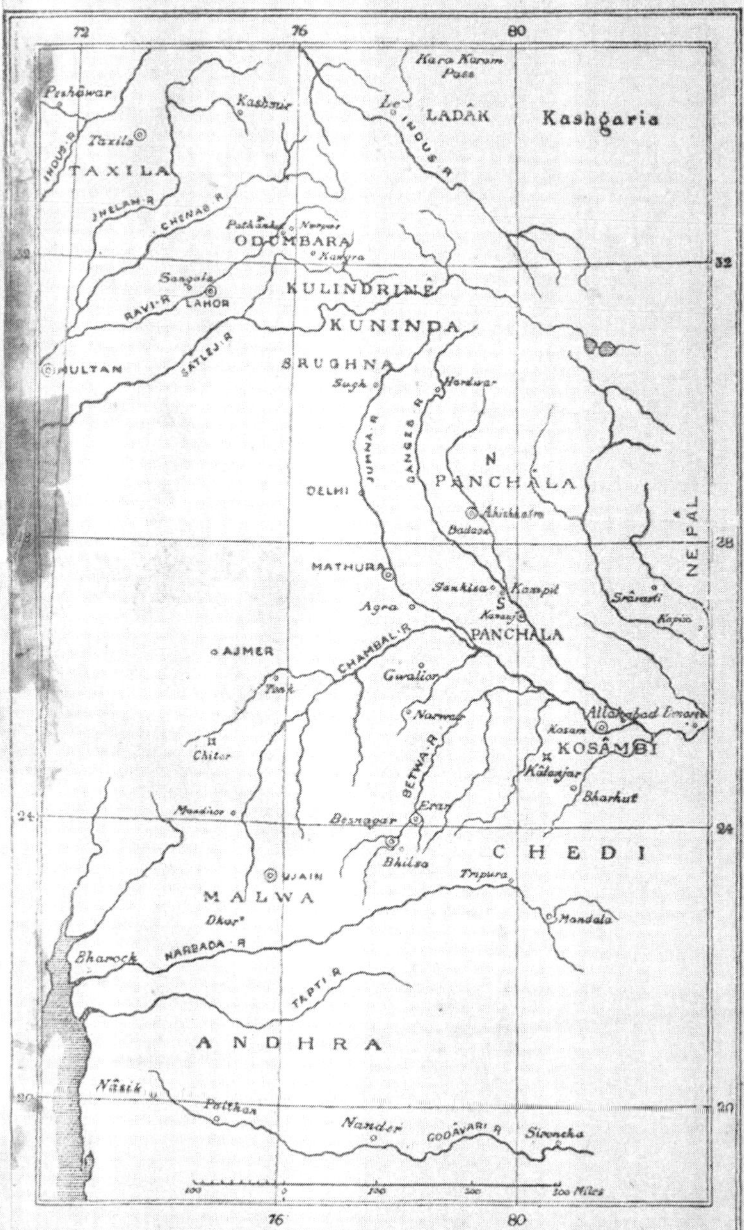

N·W - INDIA